HOW *to*
BE RICH

ALSO AVAILABLE FROM
TARCHER SUCCESS CLASSICS

JEREMY P. TARCHER/PENGUIN
a member of Penguin Group (USA) Inc.
New York

HOW *to*
BE RICH

Compact Wisdom from
the World's Greatest Wealth-Builders

INCLUDING
Napoleon Hill, Joseph Murphy,
Wallace D. Wattles,
Robert Collier, and more

Edited by

PATRICIA G. HORAN

JEREMY P. TARCHER/PENGUIN
Published by the Penguin Group
Penguin Group (USA) Inc., 375 Hudson Street, New York, New York 10014, USA •
Penguin Group (Canada), 90 Eglinton Avenue East, Suite 700, Toronto, Ontario M4P 2Y3,
Canada (a division of Pearson Penguin Canada Inc.) • Penguin Books Ltd, 80 Strand,
London WC2R 0RL, England • Penguin Ireland, 25 St Stephen's Green, Dublin 2, Ireland
(a division of Penguin Books Ltd) • Penguin Group (Australia), 250 Camberwell Road,
Camberwell, Victoria 3124, Australia (a division of Pearson Australia Group Pty Ltd) •
Penguin Books India Pvt Ltd, 11 Community Center, Panchsheel Park, New Delhi–110 017, India •
Penguin Group (NZ), 67 Apollo Drive, Rosedale, North Shore 0632, New Zealand
(a division of Pearson New Zealand Ltd) • Penguin Books (South Africa) (Pty) Ltd,
24 Sturdee Avenue, Rosebank, Johannesburg 2196, South Africa

Penguin Books Ltd, Registered Offices: 80 Strand, London WC2R 0RL, England

Most Tarcher/Penguin books are available at special quantity discounts for bulk purchase for
sales promotions, premiums, fund-raising, and educational needs. Special books or book
excerpts also can be created to fit specific needs. For details, write Penguin Group (USA) Inc.
Special Markets, 375 Hudson Street, New York, NY 10014.

Library of Congress Cataloging-in-Publication Data

How to be rich: compact wisdom from the world's greatest wealth-builders,
including Napoleon Hill, Joseph Murphy, Wallace D. Wattles, Robert Collier,
and more/edited by Patricia G. Horan.
p.   cm.
ISBN 978-1-58542-821-2
1. Success in business.   2. Wealth.   I. Horan, Patricia G.
HF5386.H577   2010   2010015347
332.024'01—dc22

Printed in the United States of America
3   5   7   9   10   8   6   4   2

Neither the publisher nor the authors are engaged in rendering professional advice or services to the
individual reader. The ideas, procedures, and suggestions contained in this book are not intended as a
substitute for consulting with a physician. All matters regarding your health require medical supervision.
Neither the authors nor the publisher shall be liable or responsible for any loss or damage allegedly arising
from any information or suggestion in this book.

While the authors have made every effort to provide accurate telephone numbers and Internet addresses at
the time of publication, neither the publisher nor the authors assume any responsibility for errors, or for
changes that occur after publication. Further, the publisher does not have any control over and does not assume
any responsibility for author or third-party websites or their content.

CONTENTS

PART II. START OVER WITH A FRIENDLY NEW ATTITUDE TOWARD WEALTH

PART III. THE ONLY ENEMIES OF OUR WEALTH LIE WITHIN

PART IV. HOW THE RICH DO IT

PART V. RECOGNIZING REAL WEALTH IS WHAT FILLS THE BANK ACCOUNT

PART VI. ATTITUDES THAT STAND BETWEEN US AND MONEY

PART VIII. SOME SIMPLE
PROSPERITY TECHNIQUES

HOW *to*
BE RICH

FOREWORD

by Patricia G. Horan

The way we measure the popularity of a subject these days is by running it through online search engines, such as Google and Amazon. If you try that with the topic of "prosperity," you'll come up with no fewer than *12 million* topic references—an astounding number—and almost 90,000 book titles on the subject. It's been proven that the less secure we are financially, and the less trust we have in outside institutions, the stronger is our desire to direct our lives ourselves, from within. As a result, popular interest in prosperity thinking is growing exponentially.

Spiritual teachers all agree that each of us is the master of our individual destinies. Through our thoughts, desires, and actions, we are molding the circumstances of our lives. The choices we make today are setting into motion the causes that will take form tomorrow as our life experiences.

To reflect on this stirring idea is to awaken to your responsibility for the conditions of your life. Ask yourself if your present life is the kind of life you most desire to live. Are you experiencing all the good you can conceive? Does your life include an abundance of the riches and wealth to which all are entitled? Are you expressing the full extent of your mental, physical and spiritual potential? If you have answered no to any of these questions, you can do something to change that condition. You can begin to incorporate into your daily routine certain ways of thinking and acting which, when practiced faithfully, will attract into your life the good you desire and deserve.

That is the exciting message of *How to Be Rich*.

How to Be Rich is a refreshing look at choice excerpts from the best motivational and prosperity material ever written. These founding geniuses of the "New Thought" movement had not yet encountered political correctness, so their messages were as direct, unlimited and powerful as their beliefs. Never have these prosperity gurus appeared together in one publication in this way. Here we see the most interesting points of the most fascinating writers, spotlighted and arranged in such a way as to support and enlighten one another. These are the writers who were inspired by such kings of fortune and discovery as the legendary Andrew Carnegie and Thomas Edison. In turn, these writers directly inspired titans such as Henry Ford.

You may not readily recognize the names of the great leaders in success whose writings appear here—such as

Napoleon Hill, Joseph Murphy, James Allen, Ralph Waldo Trine and Julia Seton. However, you will surely recognize the names of some contemporary teachers who have been inspired by them, including Wayne Dyer, Louise Hay, Tony Robbins, Dale Carnegie, Norman Vincent Peale and Deepak Chopra. Pioneering the self-help, New Thought and human potential movements, those early geniuses of success represented in this book left us an invaluable legacy. Their proven wealth-attracting steps and strategies all rest on one basic, powerful idea: *The key to everything is our thought, and we can change our life experiences only when we replace old, limited ideas with new, more expansive ones.*

In the pages that follow you will find exactly the new ideas you need to realize the riches you desire. You will find the way to wealth—and new life.

The titles and authors selected to be included here are solid gold. Among them are:

- The bestselling success book of all time, with 45 million copies sold, *Think and Grow Rich* by Napoleon Hill—the author of FDR's line "We have nothing to fear but fear itself."
- The writer whom Norman Vincent Peale likened to Thoreau, Emerson, Carnegie and Horatio Alger: Orison S. Marden.
- Arnold Bennett, one of the greatest English novelists of all time, who—it is not generally known

now—was first famous for his megaselling *Pocket Philosophies*, said to be the first series of self-help books ever published. Henry Ford bought 500 copies for his employees.

- James Allen's *As a Man Thinketh*, which has remained in print for more than 100 years, and is still selling steadily.

- Julia Seton, M.D., one of the first female members of the American Medical Association, pioneer of the holistic approach to healing.

- The book Henry Ford gave credit to for his personal success, *In Tune with the Infinite*, by Ralph Waldo Trine. This sold 2 million copies at its time of publication and inspired Hill and, later, Norman Vincent Peale.

- A brilliant author who wrote under several names and considered himself a yogi: Theron Q. Dumont, lawyer turned metaphysician, was a vital presence in the New Thought Alliance.

- Christian D. Larson, author of the famed "Optimist Creed," which to this day can be found on the walls of doctors' offices and the locker rooms of winning teams.

- The great, humble Wallace D. Wattles, whose family languished in poverty till he mastered the prosperity thinking contained in this book and brought wealth to himself and his loved ones. His inspirations ranged from Descartes and Spinoza to Swedenborg and Emerson. He is best known for his prosperity classic, *The Science of Getting Rich*.

- Dr. Joseph Murphy wrote more than thirty books. His most famous work, *The Power of Your Subconscious Mind*, which was first published in 1963, became an immediate bestseller. It was acclaimed as one of the best self-help guides ever written. Millions of copies have been sold and continue to be sold all over the world.

- Robert Collier, one of America's original self-help authors, was a prolific writer and progressive publisher who strongly believed happiness and abundance were within easy reach for all. His inspirational books have changed the lives of thousands, opening up new vistas for living fuller, richer, happier lives.

Part One

POVERTY,
NOT MONEY,
IS THE ROOT
OF ALL EVIL

WEALTH IS HEALTH. POVERTY IS THE ROOT OF ALL EVIL!

Wallace D. Wattles

Poverty is the parent of revolution and crime.

—ARISTOTLE

There is no virtue in poverty. It is a mental disease that should be abolished from the face of the earth. You are here to grow, expand and develop spiritually, mentally and materially. Some who do not prosper have a sneaky, subconscious feeling that there is some virtue in poverty. This feeling may derive from early childhood training, superstition, or be based on a false interpretation of the Scriptures.

There is no virtue in poverty. It is a disease like any other mental disease. If you were physically ill, you would think there was something wrong with you and would seek help or do something about it at once. Likewise, if you do not have money constantly circulating in your life, there is something radically wrong. God does not want you to live in a hovel or to go hungry. God *wants* you to be happy, prosperous and successful. God is always successful in divine undertakings, whether that means making a star or a cosmos.

(From *The Science of Getting Rich* by Wallace D. Wattles, 1910)

IT WAS NEVER INTENDED THAT PEOPLE SHOULD BE POOR

Theron Q. Dumont

It was never intended that people should be poor. When wealth is obtained under the proper conditions, it broadens life. Everything has a good use and a bad use. Like wealth itself, the forces of mind can be directed either for good or evil. A little rest will re-create those forces, while too much rest will degenerate into laziness and brainless, dreamy longings.

If you acquire wealth unjustly from others, then you are misusing your forces; but if your wealth comes through the right sources, you will be blessed. Through wealth we can do things to uplift ourselves and humanity.

Wealth is many people's goal. The fact is, the more attractive we make ourselves and our surroundings, the more we are prone to inspiration. It is not conducive to proper thought to be surrounded by unpleasant conditions.

(From *The Power of Concentration* by Theron Q. Dumont, 1918)

NO ONE IS DESTINED TO BE POOR: WHY WE THINK OTHERWISE

Wallace D. Wattles

No one is destined to be poor. Wealth is all around us, and all we need do to achieve it is to seek and follow the road that will lead us there.

The human race was taught that to be poor was to be spiritual, that it was "easier for the camel to go through the eye of a needle than for a rich person to enter the kingdom of Heaven." Living in this lie, they suffered on in misery, hoping and trusting that in some far-off future day, a heaven (if they deserved it by their faithful poverty) would be given them for their pain. In some religions such as those of the East, persons born in poverty will always live in poverty—

hoping that by being obedient and humble, they will be reborn in their next life in a higher caste and more afflu-ent life.

These old obsessions of race thought and race interpre-tation held the multitude in their iron clasp for centuries. Strange as it may seem, even at this late date, there are still many minds hugging to their hearts this old delusion and dragging on in penury and despair, resisting the compelling force of higher revelation. Thousands of poor people today still cling to this old tradition, only from false religious ardor and lack of self-investigation.

Many religions teach as part of their dogma that poverty is an inevitable condition for most people. They preach, "The poor will always be with us." Some sects even claim that, for many, poverty is predestined and should be accepted as a way of life.

THE BONDAGE OF
IMPOVERISHED OLD BELIEFS

The old civilization was too undeveloped to think for itself, and so for ages it accepted the thought-force of its religious and secular leaders. People built their lives to express these beliefs. As long as we believed in two forces—God and devil, spirit and matter—we received these things, for "there is nothing in this entire world but thinking makes it so." Held in the bondage of the old thoughts and beliefs, we created and re-created our own lack, limitations, disease, and poverty.

Under these teachings the multitude developed a cringing, poverty-stricken consciousness. As everything in form is projected from the inner states of consciousness, people could not escape the law they set in operation for themselves. Lack, crime, disease and abject poverty became the heritage of the human race.

THE SCIENCE OF PLANNING FOR SUCCESS

Another obsession of the old civilization is the one of inheritance. It is yet said by those who should know better: "Oh, I am born to be poor." They are born to be poor only as long as they will not, do not or cannot learn the law of supply. While there are many who are born to be poor in understanding, there are thousands who are fast working through their grade and are ready to come out into a new action of the law. The power to stand still under a law, or to go on into relationship with another, is within ourselves, but not knowing this, we stand still, accepting an old condition as binding, when within ourselves there is the awakening power for freedom.

The new civilization brings a new message. These days, many millions of people are out into a new kingdom of thought, bringing new laws into operation in their environment. Proponents of New Thought preach a new idea of life that brings out new methods and more perfected results. They base their thinking on the concept that the human soul is linked with the atomic mind of universal substance, which links our lives with the universal law of supply, and we have the power to choose how it shall manifest for us. To achieve our goals, we must work for them, and with this working suffer the thorns and heartaches of humankind. We can do all these things only as we have found the law and worked out the understanding of the law, which God seemed to have written in riddles in the past.

SOME ARE THE PROFESSIONAL POOR

The first step for the poverty-stricken is to learn to conquer supply. This conquest is brought about not from without but through the slow process of awakening individual perception, which neither the race nor the individual can outstrip. As soon as they have learned this lesson, they move on to the next step where they learn how to use wealth, and their place is immediately taken by another person learning the old lesson.

New Thought knows that there are now, and always will be, some people who accept poverty as their natural portion. However, they are not doomed to that state because the tools are there to help them lift themselves from this state by increasing development and understanding.

Those who know life understand this *first cause of poverty*. When we look more deeply, we see that until the last person of this group and similar groups has died out, the poverty-stricken will continue to be in our midst, because deep in their minds and souls they still look upon themselves as beggars. The *second cause of poverty* is the false education of the past, which, instead of hastening the evolution of humankind, has served to keep it in bondage.

We are poor and will stay poor only as long as we relate to the laws of poverty. Success, wealth and supply can be planned for by every life just as scientifically as one can build a house or plan a city. Supply cannot refuse to come to any of us who set a supply law into operation; but we must be taught this law and brought step by step away from the old ideas and obsessions of the past into a new understanding and use of new methods.

Poverty and wealth are the results of internal states of mind, and only as mind changes will material change. Environment is only a big mirror in which we see ourselves reflected. People who depend on charities for their meals or who sleep on the benches in the park are not doing so because circumstances force them to it. Due to their own ignorant manipulation of the laws, they have forced the circumstances.

Poverty will remain only as long as we have within ourselves the germ that intensifies it, and we will secure wealth and freedom only as the natural states of our minds and hearts grow into them. We are poor because we do not know any better than to be poor. We stay poor because we are too ignorant, too weak, too inert or too superstitious to hold our life servant to the higher laws of life and compel a new physical arrangement, by an ever-increasing recognition of our own God-power.

When we can fully and actually incorporate into our minds the consciousness of infinite supply, and our inseparable connection with it, we may let go of everything we have in the world and make instantaneous relation with the lines that will lead us again into abundance.

(From *The Science of Getting Rich* by Wallace D. Wattles, 1910)

Part Two

START OVER
WITH A FRIENDLY
NEW ATTITUDE
TOWARD WEALTH

YOU HAVE A RIGHT TO BE RICH, SO MAKE FRIENDS WITH MONEY

Joseph Murphy

Money has taken many forms as a medium of exchange down through the centuries, such as salt, beads and trinkets of various kinds. In early times wealth was determined by the number of sheep and oxen one had. Now we use currency, and other negotiable instruments, as it is much more convenient to write a check than carry some sheep around with you to pay bills.

It is your right to be rich. You are here to lead the abundant life and be happy, radiant and free. You should, therefore, have all the money you need to lead a full, happy and prosperous life. You are here to grow, expand and unfold spiritually, mentally and materially.

Why be satisfied with just enough to go around when you can enjoy the riches of your subconscious mind? You can learn to make friends with money, and you should always have a surplus. Your desire to be rich is a desire for a fuller, happier, more wonderful life. It is a cosmic urge. *It is not only good, but very good.*

Cleanse your mind of all weird and superstitious beliefs about money. Do not ever regard money as evil or filthy. If you do, you cause it to take wings and fly away from you. Remember that you lose what you condemn. You cannot attract what you criticize.

(From *The Power of Your Subconscious Mind* by Joseph Murphy, 1963)

ANOTHER LOOK AT MAKING FRIENDS WITH MONEY

Wallace D. Wattles

There is nothing wrong in wanting to get rich. The desire for riches is really the desire for a richer, fuller and more abundant life; and that desire is praiseworthy. People who do not desire to live more abundantly are abnormal, and so people who do not desire to have enough money to buy all they want are abnormal. You have the inalienable right to fully develop and express yourself along all lines. You should surround yourself with beauty and luxury. Why be satisfied with just enough to go around when you can enjoy the riches of the infinite? Make friends with money.

There are three motives for which we live: we live for the body; we live for the mind; we live for the soul. No one of these is better or holier than the other. All are equally desirable, and no one of the three—body, mind or soul—can live fully if either of the others is cut short of full life and expression. It is not right or noble to live only for the soul and deny mind or body; and it is wrong to live for the intellect and deny body or soul. We are all acquainted with the loathsome consequences of living for the body and denying both mind and soul; and we see that real life means the complete expression of all that we can give forth through body, mind and soul.

(From *The Science of Getting Rich* by Wallace D. Wattles, 1910)

YOU CAN'T ENJOY WHAT YOU DESPISE

Wallace D. Wattles

One of the reasons why many people do not have more money is that they are silently or openly condemning it. They refer to money as "filthy lucre" or say, "The love of money is the root of all evil."

A man once said to me, "I am broke. I do not like money. It is the root of all evil." These statements represent a confused, neurotic mind. Love of money to the exclusion of everything else will cause you to become lopsided and unbalanced. You are here to use your power or authority wisely. Some crave power; others crave money. If you set your heart on money exclusively and say, "Money is all I want; I am going to give all my attention to amassing money; nothing else matters," you can get money and attain a fortune, but you have forgotten that you are here to lead a balanced life. You must also satisfy the hunger for peace of mind, harmony, love, joy and perfect health.

Suppose, for example, you found gold, silver, lead, copper or iron in the ground. Would you pronounce these things evil? All evil comes from man's darkened understanding, from his ignorance, from his false interpretation of life and from his misuse of his subconscious mind. Uranium, lead or some other metal could have been used as a medium of exchange. We use paper notes, checks, nickel and silver. Surely these are not evil.

(From *The Science of Getting Rich* by Wallace D. Wattles, 1910)

INSULTING THE RICH IS SAYING YOU DON'T WANT TO JOIN THEM

Wallace D. Wattles

Get away immediately from all superstitious beliefs about money. Do not ever regard money as evil or filthy. If you do, you cause it to take wings and fly away from you. Remember that you lose what you condemn. Begin to see money in its true significance. It is a symbol of exchange. It means to you freedom from want, beauty, luxury, abundance and refinement.

(From *The Science of Getting Rich* by Wallace D. Wattles, 1910)

BETTER NOT CONDEMN THE
VERY THING YOU PRAY FOR

Joseph Murphy

I am sure you have heard men say, "That fellow has a racket." "He is a racketeer." "He is getting money dishonestly." "He is a faker." "I knew him when he had nothing." "He is a crook, a thief and a swindler."

If you analyze the man who talks like that, you discover he is usually in want or suffering from some financial or physical illness. Perhaps his former college friends went up the ladder of success and excelled him. Now he is bitter and envious of their progress. In many instances this is the cause of his downfall. Thinking negatively of these classmates and condemning their wealth causes the wealth and prosperity he is praying for to vanish and flee away. He is condemning the thing he is praying for.

He is praying in two ways. On the one hand he is saying, "Wealth is flowing to me now," and in the next breath, silently or audibly, he is saying, "I resent that fellow's wealth." Always make it a special point to rejoice in the wealth of the other person.

(From *The Power of Your Subconscious Mind* by Joseph Murphy, 1963)

WHAT WE ARE SEEKING IS SEEKING US: THE MIND AS MAGNET

Julia Seton

When we know this truth of the law of Divine Transference, we just lift our minds above the thought world of effort and resistance, high above the planes of recognition of competition. We neither know nor care what the external conditions may be; we only know what we want, and know how, and when, and where, we want it. We forget that there is any condition that might have power over us. We know that God wants us to have what we want, and we know that it is waiting for us in the creative energy, ready to burst into bloom for us the moment we make continuous connection with it. God has provided some better things for us, and through us they can be made perfect.

When we get this New Thought position and have a business, it will increase along every line. If we want a new position or want to change our present work, we are so full of the knowledge of our own power and the abundant supply of everything that we want, that when we go out to ask for one thing, a dozen other things come along with it just because we are so full of a divine attraction which our conscious recognition has built into our life. We know, then, that the thing we seek is seeking us, and we go out to meet it, fully expecting to see it meet us halfway. Then over our own external line of connection our abundance comes. We may inherit it, attract it, marry it, work for it but come it must, and over any line we declare for ourselves, it is for us to command, form must obey. In this new line of transference we never take anything from another. We cannot do that anyway; even on the plane of competition, the law is that the thing we seek and our point of attraction must be equal, or it passes us and cleaves to the one who is strong enough to claim it physically, mentally or ethically. But under this higher law of recognition the lines never cross; everything finds its own place, and we get the entire thing on a plane of consciousness so high that we have undisputed possession of it.

When we first come into the law of this plane of Divine Transference, we feel as if we were magnets attracting to us, from an unlimited source, these things we desire. However, after a while even this much separation ceases and we feel that we are the *abundance itself,* the *law* and the *Transference.* We are *it, All* in *all,* and are out into the kingdom of cosmic dominion. Our whole world environment becomes the picture of the wealth and abundance that we have earned for ourselves by our deepened consciousness.

We let go of longings, hopes, fears and anxieties and just

become one in realization with the abundance of universal supply; this must end for us in actualization on our material plane.

This is the great cosmic law from which there is no appeal. When we make our whole attitude one of divine recognition of opulence, everything we desire will come from out of the external world around us and attach itself to our lives, and we shall express the fullness of peace and power and plenty. We cease then to look to others, but rather to substance itself for our supply. Others may refuse to pay, but the law of supply never refuses; it pays today, tomorrow and for ever. Others must pay, when the law has spoken.

(From *The Science of Success* by Julia Seton, 1914)

Part Three

THE ONLY ENEMIES
OF OUR WEALTH
LIE WITHIN

WATCH YOUR THOUGHTS:
HATE WITHIN, HOVEL WITHOUT

Wallace D. Wattles

You are only really injured by what is in you.

—JAMES ALLEN

There are childish states of consciousness that operate against material harmony. Worry, hate, fear, anxiety and condemnation are interior pivots for exterior hovels. Wherever we rest our ideas and energies, substance must gather round. "Envy is the ulcer of the soul," said Socrates.

A mind that has been poised through incarnations in the belief of poverty and its power, and backs this belief in the present with childish states of mind—anger, worry and fear—will find poverty abiding with it.

(From *The Science of Getting Rich* by Wallace D. Wattles, 1910)

THERE ARE NO SECRET THOUGHTS

James Allen

*Our destiny changes with our thought. We shall become
what we wish to become, do what we wish to do, when
our habitual thought corresponds with our desire.*

—O. S. MARDEN

L et us radically alter our thoughts, and we will be astonished at the rapid transformation it will effect in the material conditions of our lives. We may imagine that thought can be kept secret, but it cannot; it rapidly crystallizes into habit, and habit solidifies into circumstance. Bestial thoughts crystallize into habits of drunkenness and sensuality, which solidify into circumstances of destitution and disease.

Impure thoughts of every kind crystallize into enervating and confusing habits, which solidify into distracting and adverse circumstances.

Thoughts of fear, doubt and indecision crystallize into weak, soft and irresolute habits, which solidify into circumstances of failure, indigence and slavish dependence.

Lazy thoughts crystallize into habits of unseemliness and

dishonesty, which solidify into circumstances of disgust and beggary.

Hateful and condemnatory thoughts crystallize into habits of accusation and violence, which solidify into circumstances of injury and persecution.

Selfish thoughts of all kinds crystallize into habits of self-seeking, which solidify into circumstances more or less distressing.

On the other hand, beautiful thoughts of all kinds crystallize into habits of grace and kindliness, which solidify into genial and sunny circumstances.

Pure thoughts crystallize into habits of temperance and self-control, which solidify into circumstances of repose and peace.

Thoughts of courage, self-reliance and decision crystallize into strong habits, which solidify into circumstances of success, plenty and freedom.

Energetic thoughts crystallize into habits of cleanliness and industry, which solidify into circumstances of pleasantness.

Gentle and forgiving thoughts crystallize into habits of gentleness, which solidify into protective and preservative circumstances.

Loving and unselfish thoughts crystallize into habits of self-forgetfulness for others, which solidify into circumstances of sure and abiding prosperity and true riches.

A particular train of thought persisted in, whether it is

good or bad, cannot fail to produce its results on the character and circumstances. We cannot directly choose our circumstances, but we can choose our thoughts, and so indirectly, yet surely, shape our circumstances.

Nature helps us to the gratification of encouraging thoughts, and opportunities are presented which will most speedily bring to the surface both the good and evil thoughts.

Let us cease from our negative thoughts, and all the world will soften toward us, and be ready to help us. Put away weak and sickly thoughts, and opportunities will spring up on every hand to aid our strong resolves. Encourage good thoughts, and no hard fate will drag us down to wretchedness and shame.

The world is our kaleidoscope, and the varying combinations of colors, which at every succeeding moment it presents to us, are the exquisitely adjusted pictures of our ever-moving thoughts.

(From *As a Man Thinketh* by James Allen, 1903)

DON'T TRY TO CREATE WEALTH WITH POVERTY THOUGHTS

Wallace D. Wattles

You cannot retain a true and clear vision of wealth if you are constantly turning your attention to opposing pictures, whether they are external or imaginary.

Do not talk about your past troubles of a financial nature, if you have had them. Do not think of them at all. Do not tell of the poverty of your parents or the hardships of your early life. To do any of these things is to mentally class yourself with the poor for the time being, and it will certainly check the movement of things in your direction.

"Let the dead bury their dead." Put poverty and all things that pertain to poverty completely behind you.

You have now accepted a certain theory of the universe as being correct and are resting all your hopes of happiness on its being correct. What can you gain by giving heed to conflicting theories?

Do not read books that tell you that the world is soon coming to an end; and do not read the writing of pessimistic philosophers who tell you that it is going to the devil. The world is not going to the devil; it is going to God.

True, there may be a good many things in existing conditions that are disagreeable; but what is the use of studying them when they are certainly passing away, and when the study of them only tends to check their passing and keep them with us? Why give time and attention to things that are being removed by evolutionary growth, when you can hasten their removal only by promoting the evolutionary growth as far as your part of it goes?

THINK ABOUT THE WORLD BECOMING RICH

No matter how horrible-seeming may be the conditions in certain countries, sections or places, you waste your time and destroy your own chances by considering them. You should interest yourself in the world becoming rich.

Think of the riches the world is coming into, instead of the poverty it is growing out of. Bear in mind that the only way in which you can assist the world in growing rich is by growing rich yourself through the creative method—not the competitive one.

Give your attention wholly to riches; ignore poverty. Whenever you think or speak of those who are poor, think and speak of them as those who are becoming rich, as those who are to be congratulated rather than pitied. Then they and others will catch the inspiration and begin to search for the way out.

Because you give your whole time and mind and thought to riches, it does not follow that you are to be sordid or mean. To become really rich is the noblest aim you can have in life, for it includes everything else. On the competitive plane, the struggle to get rich is a godless scramble for power over others; but when we come into the creative mind, all this is changed.

All that is possible in the way of greatness and development of your soul, of service and lofty endeavor, comes by way of getting rich; all is made possible by the use of things. If you lack for physical health, you will find that the attainment of it is conditional on your getting rich. Only those who are emancipated from financial worry and have the means to live a carefree existence and follow hygienic practices can have and retain health.

GREATNESS IS ONLY FOR
THE NONCOMPETITIVE

Moral and spiritual greatness is possible only to those who are above the competitive battle for existence. Only those who are becoming rich on the plane of creative thought are free from the degrading influences of competition. If your heart is set on domestic happiness, remember that love flourishes best where there is refinement, a high level of thought, and freedom from corrupting influences; and these are to be found only where riches are attained by the exercise of creative thought, without strife or rivalry.

You can aim at nothing so great or noble as to become rich; and you must fix your attention upon your mental picture of riches, to the exclusion of all that may tend to dim or obscure the vision. You must learn to see the underlying *truth* in all things. You must see beneath all seemingly wrong conditions that life is ever moving forward toward fuller expression and more complete happiness.

It is the truth that there is no such thing as poverty—that there is only wealth. Some people remain in poverty because they are ignorant of the fact that there is wealth for them. These people can best be taught by showing them the way to affluence in your own person and practice.

Others are poor because, while they feel that there is a way out, they are too intellectually indolent to put forth the mental effort necessary to find that way and travel it. For these the very best thing you can do is to arouse their desire by showing them the happiness that comes from being rightly rich.

HELP THE WORLD BY HELPING YOURSELF

Others still are poor because, while they have some notion of science, they have become so swamped and lost in the maze of metaphysical and occult theories that they do not know which road to take. They try a mixture of many systems and fail in all. For these, again, the very best thing to do is to show the right way in your own person and practice. An ounce of doing things is worth a pound of theorizing.

The very best thing you can do for the whole world is to make the most of yourself. You can serve God and humankind in no more effective way than by getting rich; that is, if you get rich by the creative method and not by the competitive one.

(From *The Science of Getting Rich* by Wallace D. Wattles, 1910)

Part Four

How the Rich
Do It

THE ART OF WELCOMING WEALTH

Theron Q. Dumont

The first step toward acquiring wealth is to surround yourself with helpful influences—to claim for yourself an environment of culture; to place yourself in it and be molded by its influences.

Most great people of all ages have been comparatively rich. They have made or inherited money. Without money they could not have accomplished what they did. Those engaged in physical drudgery are not likely to have the same high ideals as those who can command comparative leisure.

One of the big mistakes made by many people is to associate with those who fail to develop the best that is in them. When people develop a social life too exclusively, and recreation or entertainment becomes their leading motive, they acquire habits of extravagance instead of economy— habits of wasting physical, mental, moral and spiritual resources instead of conserving them. They lose motivation and God-given powers, and their forces remain undeveloped. This inevitably brings bad judgment to bear upon all the higher relationships of life, creating lean fortunes, culturally and financially. Often a parasite, such a person is as heavy a consumer as he or she is a poor producer.

It seems a tragedy that these people have to learn such painful lessons before they can understand the forces and laws that regulate life. Few profit by the mistakes of others. They must experience them for themselves and then apply the knowledge in reconstructing their lives.

Anyone who has ever amounted to anything has never done a great deal of detailed work for long periods at any given time. He or she needs time to reflect. The successful do not perform duties today in the same way as yesterday. As the result of deliberate and concentrated effort, they constantly try to improve working methods.

LECTURING ON PROSPERITY IN POOR SURROUNDINGS!

The other day I attended a lecture on prosperity. I knew the lecturer had been practically broke for 10 years. I wanted to hear what he had to say. He spoke very well, and no doubt he benefited some of his listeners, but somehow he had not profited by his own teachings. I introduced myself and asked him if he believed in his maxims. He said he did. I asked him if they had made him prosperous. He said not exactly. I asked him why. He answered that he thought he was fated not to experience prosperity.

In half an hour I showed that man why poverty had always been his companion. He had dressed poorly. He held his lectures in poor surroundings. By his actions and beliefs he attracted poverty. *He did not realize that his thoughts and surroundings exercised an unfavorable influence on him.*

"Thoughts are moving forces and great powers," I said. "Thoughts of wealth attract wealth. Therefore, if you desire wealth you must attract the forces that will help you secure it. Your thoughts attract similar thoughts. If you hold thoughts of poverty, you attract poverty. If you make up your mind that you are going to be wealthy, you will instill this thought into all your mental forces, and you will at the same time use every external condition to help you."

THOUGHT, NOT MONEY, MAKES MONEY

Many people are of the opinion that if you have money it is easy to make more. This is not necessarily true. Ninety percent of people who start a business fail. Money will not enable one to accumulate more unless he or she is trained to seek and use good opportunities for its investment. If one inherits money, the chances are that it will be lost.

What we take from others will, in turn, be taken from us. All obligations have to be met fairly and squarely. We cannot reach perfection until we discharge every obligation of our lives. We all realize this, so why not willingly give a fair exchange for all that we receive?

I repeat that the first as well as the last step in acquiring wealth is to surround yourself with good influences—good thought, good health, good home and business environment and successful business associates. Cultivate, by every legitimate means, the acquaintance of high-caliber people. Bring your business thoughts into harmony with theirs. This will make your society not only agreeable, but sought-after; and, when you have formed intimate friendships with reputable, wealthy business people, entrust them with your surplus earnings for investment until you have developed the initiative and business acumen to successfully manage your own investments. When your fortune is secured, you will then take pleasure in using a part of it in making the road you traveled easier for those who follow you.

Somewhere in your brain is the energy that will get you out of that rut and place you high on the mountain of success if you can only use the energy. The gasoline in your engine won't move your car until a spark ignites it. So it is with your mind. Everyone has the capacity to climb over the word "impossible" and get into the successful country beyond. Hope, self-confidence and determination supply the spark that makes your energy work.

(From *The Power of Concentration* by Theron Q. Dumont, 1918)

AFFIRM ALWAYS, "THERE IS NO POVERTY," DESPITE APPEARANCES

Wallace D. Wattles

There is no labor from which most people shrink as they do from that of sustained and consecutive thought; it is the hardest work in the world. This is especially true when truth is contrary to appearances. Every appearance in the visible world tends to produce a corresponding form in the mind that observes it—and this can only be prevented by holding the thought of the *truth*.

To look upon the appearances of poverty will produce corresponding forms in your own mind, unless you hold to the truth that there is no poverty—there is only abundance. To think riches when in the midst of appearances of poverty requires power. Those who acquire this power become masterminds who can conquer fate and can have what they want.

This power can only be acquired by getting hold of the basic fact that is behind all appearances. That fact is that there is one Thinking Substance, from which and by which all things are made. Then we must grasp the truth that every thought held in this substance becomes a form, and that we can so impress our thoughts upon it as to cause them to take form and become visible things. When we realize this, we lose all doubt and fear, for we know that we can create what we want to create; we can get what we want to have, and can become what we want to be.

(From *The Science of Getting Rich* by Wallace D. Wattles, 1910)

CREATE WEALTH, INSTEAD OF COMPETING FOR IT

Christian D. Larson

Do not believe it when the world tells you to step over others to succeed. Those who practice this will find one day that everyone they know has deserted them. When they call out in anguish and loneliness, no one will hear them.

To consider one's self before all others is to warp every noble and divine impulse. Let your soul expand. Let your heart reach out to others in loving and generous warmth. If you do this, your life will have great and lasting joy. Prosperity will seek you out.

Riches secured by destructive competition are never satisfactory and permanent; they are yours today, and another's tomorrow. Remember, if you are to become rich in a scientific and certain way, you must rise entirely out of the competitive thought. You must never think for a moment that the supply is limited.

Know that there are countless millions of dollars' worth of treasure in the mountains of the earth, not yet brought to light; and know that if there were not, more would be created from Thinking Substance to supply your needs.

Know that the money you need will come, even if it is necessary for a thousand people to be led to the discovery of new resources tomorrow.

Never look at the visible supply; look always at the limitless riches in Divine Substance, and *know* that they are coming to you as fast as you can receive and use them. Nobody, by cornering the visible supply, can prevent you from getting what is yours.

So never allow yourself to think for an instant that all the best building spots will be taken before you get ready to build your house, unless you hurry. Never worry about the conglomerates and cartels, and get anxious for fear they will soon come to own the whole earth. Never get afraid that you will lose what you want because some other person "beats you to it." That cannot possibly happen; you are not seeking anything that is possessed by anybody else; you are causing what you want to be created from Divine Substance, and the supply is without limits.

(From *Your Forces and How to Use Them* by Christian D. Larson, 1912)

WHY DOING *MORE* WORK THAN WE'RE PAID FOR LEADS TO WEALTH

Napoleon Hill

This law is a stumbling block, and many a promising career has been broken on it. There is a general inclination among people to perform just as little work as they can get by with. But if you will study these people carefully, you will observe that while they may be actually "getting by" temporarily, they are also not getting anything else!

There are two major reasons why all successful people must practice this law:

1. Just as an arm or a limb of the body grows strong in exact proportion to its use, so does the mind grow strong through use. By rendering the greatest possible amount of service, the faculties through which the service is rendered are put into greater use, becoming strong and accurate.

2. By rendering more service than that for which you are paid, you will be turning the spotlight of favorable attention upon yourself, and it will not

be long before you will be sought after, with impressive offers for your services.

"Do the thing and you shall have the power" was the admonition of Emerson, to this day our greatest philosopher. That is literally true! Practice makes perfect. The better you do your work, the more adept you become at doing it, and this, in time, will lead to such perfection that you will have few, if any, equals in your field.

ENJOY THE LAW OF INCREASING RETURNS

By rendering more service and better service than that for which you are paid, you thereby take advantage of the Law of Increasing Returns. This means that you will eventually be paid, in one way or another, for far more service than you actually perform.

This is not just an attractive theory. It actually works out in the most practical tests. You must not imagine, however, that this law always works instantaneously. You may render more service and better service than you are supposed to render for a few days, then discontinue the practice and go back to the old, usual habit of doing as little as can be safely trusted to get you by, and the results will in no way benefit you. But if you adopt the habit as a part of your life's philosophy, and let it become known by all who know you that you render such service out of choice—not as a matter of accident, but by deliberate intent—you will soon see keen competition for your service.

You'll observe that it's not easy to find very many people rendering such service, which is all the better for you, because you will stand out in bold contrast with practically all others who are engaged in work similar to yours. Contrast is a powerful law, and you may, in this manner, profit by contrast.

Some people set up the weak but popular argument that it does not pay to render more service and better service than one is paid for because it is not appreciated. They add that they work for people who are selfish and will not recognize such service. Splendid! The more selfish an employer is, the more inclined he or she will be to continue to employ a person who makes a point of rendering such service, which is unusual both in quantity and quality. This very selfishness will impel such an employer to recognize such services. However, if the employer should happen to lack the necessary vision, then it is only a matter of time until all who render such service will attract the attention of other employers who will gladly reward them.

Careful study of the lives of successful people has shown that faithfully practicing this one law alone has brought the compensations with which success is usually measured. If the author of this philosophy had to choose one of the 17 Laws of Success as being the most important, and had to discard all the others except the one chosen, he would, without a moment's hesitation, choose this Law of Rendering More Service and Better Service Than Paid For.

(From *The Magic Ladder to Success* by Napoleon Hill, 1930)

GIVE YOUR BUSINESS ALL YOU'VE GOT, AND MORE

Robert Collier

I f you want more of the universal supply, you must use that which you have in such a way as to make yourself of greater service to those around you.

"Whosoever shall be great among you," said Jesus, "shall be your minister, and whosoever of you will be the chiefs, shall be servant of all." In other words, if you would be great, you must serve. And he who serves most shall be greatest of all. If you want to make more money, instead of seeking it for yourself, see how you can make more for others. In the process you will inevitably make more for yourself, too. We get as we give—but we must give first.

It matters not where you start—you may be a day laborer— but still you can give: give a bit more of energy, of work, of thought than you are paid for. "Whosoever shall compel thee to go a mile," said Jesus, "go with him twain." Try to put a little extra skill into your work. Use your mind to find some better way of doing whatever task may be set for you. It won't be long before you are out of the common working class. There is no kind of work that cannot be bettered by thought. There is no method that cannot be improved by thought. So give generously of your thought to your work. Think every minute you are at it: "Isn't there some way in which this could be done easier, quicker, better?"

The true spirit of business is the spirit of that plucky old Danish sea captain, Peter Tordenskjold. Attacked by a Swedish frigate, after all his crew but one had been killed and his supply of cannon balls was exhausted, Peter boldly kept up the fight, firing pewter dinner plates and mugs from his one remaining gun. One of the pewter mugs hit the Swedish captain and killed him, and Peter sailed off triumphant! Look around you now. How can *you* give greater value for what you get? How can you better serve? How can you make more money for your employers or save more for your customers? Keep that thought ever in the forefront of your mind and you'll never need to worry about making more for yourself!

(From *The Secret of the Ages* by Robert Collier, 1926)

IN ORDER TO *GET*, WE MUST *GIVE*

Ralph Waldo Trine

We may become wealthy, very wealthy in the sense of acquiring money. We may become billionaires by working for it directly. But very common people have done that. Indeed, many of a low type have done it. We now have sense enough not to call these great people. Careful analysis will show, in every case, that greatness in a man or woman requires service to others. The one who is working for greatness alone is the one who ordinarily never achieves it.

One of the great laws of life is giving—we term it "service." Service for others is just as essential to our real happiness and to our highest welfare as is our work for our own individual welfare. We do not live for ourselves alone. No one *can*. The Order of the Universe has been written from time immemorial against it.

There is no one who has ever found happiness by striving for it directly. It never has and it never can come that way. Why? Simply because the very laws of the universe are against it.

It was Charles Kingsley who sang so truly:

Friends, in this world of hurry
And work and sudden end,
If a thought comes quick of doing
A kindness to a friend,
Do it that very instant!
Don't put it off—don't wait!
What's the use of doing a kindness
If you do it a day too late!

It is the one who has mind and heart centered on accomplishing the thing that is of service who may someday be elevated by the silent vote to the position of greatness. So, there is no such thing as finding happiness by seeking for it directly. It comes always through the operation of a great and universally established law—by the sympathy, the care, the consideration we render to others.

ONLY THOSE WHO SERVE ARE WORTHY OF SUCCESS

The higher types of happiness will never come by seeking for them directly. It is a real interest in the affairs of others that makes for a generous, wholesome, inclusive and, therefore, broad and happy life. The life that is sharing in the interests, the welfare and the happiness of others is the one that is continually expanding in beauty and in power and, therefore, in happiness. The little, the equivocal, the small, the exclusive, the pure self-seeker are never among those genuinely happy. As Henry Drummond once said, they are on the wrong track. The large-hearted, the sympathetic, those always ready with the helping hand are the ones who have found the road.

Joy in another's success not only indicates those of the big-hearted type, but it indicates that they in turn are worthy of success themselves. And if they are not always what we term a success in some given field, or art, or in acquiring wealth, they are a success in the greatest of arts, the Art of Living. *They are also a success in that the joy and happiness of others enters into and becomes a portion of their own lives.* Half the heartaches of the world would be banished, and half its burdens would be lifted, if every life were habitually tuned to this deep but simply expressed sentiment by Emily Dickinson:

> *They might not need me—yet they might,*
> *I'll let my heart be just in sight.*
> *A smile so small as mine might be*
> *Precisely their necessity.*

(From *The Winning of the Best* by Ralph Waldo Trine, 1912)

TRUE WEALTH IS FOUND IN SERVICE

Ralph Waldo Trine

I am well aware of the fact that the mere accumulation of wealth is not, except in very rare cases, the controlling motive in the lives of the wealthy. It is rather the joy and the satisfaction of achievement. But nevertheless it is possible, as has so often been proved, to get so much into a habit and thereby into a rut that one becomes a victim of habit. Then life, with all its superb possibilities of human service—and therefore of true greatness—becomes sidetracked and abortive. Greatness comes always through human service. As there is no such thing as *finding* happiness by searching for it directly, so there is no such thing as achieving greatness by seeking it directly. It comes not primarily through brilliant intellect, great talents, but primarily through the heart. It is determined by the way that brilliant intellect and great talents are used. It is accorded not to those who seek it directly. By an indirect law, it is accorded to those who, forgetting self, give and thereby lose their lives in human service.

(From *Higher Powers of Mind and Spirit* by Ralph Waldo Trine, 1918)

TO PROSPER, LET NO ONE CONTROL YOU

Christian D. Larson

Since the principle of complete control exists within us, there is a way to apply that principle in everything, and at all times. But to be successful in this, the attitude of self-supremacy must prevail at all times, and under all conditions.

When we live in this attitude of self-supremacy, we exercise complete control over certain things in our lives; but when we hold the belief that we are controlled or influenced by other things, we abandon the attitude of self-supremacy, and cease to exercise complete control over our lives.

In the present state of human development, the average mind is so constituted that it swings from one state to another, remaining the greater part of the time in the attitude of self-submission. This is because we are seldom absolutely true to our higher convictions, and also because we try to think that both beliefs are true at the same time. Consequently, the great essential for us in our present state is to accept the highest conviction as an absolute truth, and be true to that truth every moment of existence.

To be true to that truth, we must absolutely refuse to be-

lieve that we can be controlled or influenced by anything
or anybody. We must depart completely from the belief in
control by other powers, and must recognize in ourselves the
only power to completely control everything in our own
domain.

Nor is this a contradiction, because when we enter the
consciousness of self-supremacy, we cannot submit ourselves
to any outside influence; therefore there are no outside influences in action in our lives. And when this is the case, we
cannot believe in the existence of outside influences, to the
extent of believing that nothing is trying to control us, so
that we cannot truthfully say that we are being controlled,
or ever will be.

When we are in this state of self-supremacy, we are in
a state where no influence from without exists; we are in a
world where the power of self-mastery is the only controlling power; therefore, we cannot truthfully recognize any
other control.

While in the attitude of self-submission, on the other
hand, your mind is open to all kinds of impressions from
without, and consequently your thinking will be suggested
to you by your environment. The result is that you will become like your environment, and will think, act and live as
your environment may suggest.

If your environment is inferior, you will think inferior
thoughts, live an inferior life and commit deeds that are
low or perverse, as long as you are in the attitude of self-

submission. But if you should submit yourself to a better environment, your life, thoughts and deeds would naturally become better. In each case you would be the representation of the impressions that enter through the senses.

PRACTICE THE ART OF ORIGINAL THINKING

With such a passive attitude, the very moment you pass from a superior environment to one that is inferior, you will begin to change for the worse, unless you have in the meantime attained a degree of self-supremacy. To enter a superior environment will not of itself develop self-supremacy or the art of original thinking, because as long as you permit yourself to be influenced by environment, you prevent your mind from gaining consciousness of the principle of self-supremacy. A change of environment, therefore, will not give us the power to master our fate. This power comes only through a change of thought.

While in the attitude of self-supremacy, your mind is not open to impressions from any source, but you can place your mind, at will, in the responsive attitude, so that it may receive impressions from any source that you may select. By proper selection, consciousness can, in this way, be trained to express itself only through those mental channels that reach the superior side of things, and thereby come in contact with *the unlimited possibilities* of things. Through contact with unlimited possibilities, your mind will be able to form original thoughts that embody superior powers and attainments, and as you become like your thoughts, you will, through this process, become superior.

BUILDING YOUR LARGER LIFE

Instead of being controlled by the impressions received from your environment, you will control those impressions, and use them as material in the construction of your own larger life, and the greater destiny that must follow.

While your mind is in the attitude of self-supremacy, your contact with the world will not affect you in any way but the way you desire to be affected. This is because you control the impressions that come from without, and can completely change the natures of these impressions before they are accepted in consciousness. Or you may refuse to accept them entirely.

In the midst of adversity do not permit the negativity of the circumstances to impress your mind, but open your mind to be impressed by the great power that is hidden within the adversity. Our mind is not impressed by the misdirection of power, but by the power itself. Therefore, instead of being disturbed, you are made stronger. There is something of value to be gained from every disagreeable condition, because within every condition there is power, and there are always greater hidden possibilities than the surface indicates. Through original thinking these greater possibilities are discerned, and when mind is in the attitude of self-supremacy, it may choose to be impressed by the greater possibilities only, thus providing more material for our reconstruction, and our destiny, on a larger and superior scale.

It is therefore evident that self-supremacy is indispensable, and it is attained by basing all life, all thought and all action upon the principle that we are inherently master over everything in our lives, and by refusing absolutely to believe that we can be controlled by environment under any condition whatever.

(From *Mastery of Fate* by Christian D. Larson, 1910)

BURN YOUR BRIDGES IN THE HEAT OF YOUR DESIRE

Napoleon Hill

When Edwin C. Barnes climbed down from a freight train in Orange, New Jersey, he may have resembled a tramp, but his thoughts were those of a king! As he made his way from the railway line to Thomas A. Edison's office, his mind was at work. He saw himself *standing in Edison's presence*. He heard himself asking Mr. Edison for an opportunity to carry out the one CONSUMING OBSESSION OF HIS LIFE, a BURNING DESIRE to become the business associate of the great inventor.

Barnes's desire was not a hope! It was not a wish! It was a keen, pulsating DESIRE, which transcended everything else. It was DEFINITE. The desire was not new when he approached Edison. It had been Barnes's dominating desire for a long time. In the beginning, when the desire first appeared in his mind, it may have been, probably was, only a wish, but it was no mere wish when he appeared before Edison with it.

A few years later, Edwin C. Barnes again stood before Edison, in the same office where he first met the inventor. This time his DESIRE had been translated into reality. He was in business with Edison. The dominating DREAM OF HIS LIFE had become a reality. Today, people who know Barnes envy him because of the "break" life yielded him. They see him in the days of his triumph, without taking the trouble to investigate the cause of his success.

Barnes succeeded because he chose a definite goal and placed all his energy, all his willpower and all his effort—everything—behind that goal. He did not become the partner of Edison the day he arrived. He was content to start in the most menial work, as long as it provided an opportunity to take even one step toward his cherished goal.

Five years passed before the chance he had been seeking

made its appearance. During all those years, not one ray of hope, not one promise of attainment of his DESIRE had been held out to him. To everyone except himself he appeared as only another cog in the Edison business wheel, but in his own mind HE WAS THE PARTNER OF EDISON EVERY MINUTE OF THE TIME, from the very day that he first went to work there.

It is a remarkable illustration of the power of a DEFINITE DESIRE. Barnes won his goal because he wanted to be a business associate of Mr. Edison more than he wanted anything else. He created a plan by which to attain that purpose. But he BURNED ALL BRIDGES BEHIND HIM. He stood by his DESIRE until it became the dominating obsession of his life and, finally, a fact.

When he went to Orange, he did not say to himself, "I will try to induce Edison to give me a job of some sort." He said, "I will see Edison, and put him on notice that I have come to go into business with him."

He did not say, "I will work there for a few months, and if I get no encouragement, I will quit and get a job somewhere else." He did say, "I will start anywhere. I will do anything Edison tells me to do, but before I am through, I will be his associate." He did not say, "I will keep my eyes open for another opportunity, in case I fail to get what I want in the Edison organization." He said, "There is but ONE thing in this world that I am determined to have, and that is a business association with Thomas A. Edison. I will burn all bridges behind me, and stake my ENTIRE FUTURE on my ability to get what I want."

He left himself no possible way of retreat. He had to win or perish! That is all there is to the Barnes story of success!

(From *Think and Grow Rich* by Napoleon Hill, 1937)

Part Five

RECOGNIZING REAL WEALTH IS WHAT FILLS THE BANK ACCOUNT

EVERY MAGIC MORNING OUR
PURSE OF TIME IS FILLED

Arnold Bennett

Newspapers are full of articles explaining how to live on such and such an amount. Recently, in a daily paper, a battle raged over the question of whether a woman can exist nicely in the country on £85 a year. I have seen an essay, "How to live on eight shillings a week." But I have never seen an essay, "How to live on 24 hours a day."

Yet it has been said that time is money. That proverb understates the case. Time is a great deal more than money. If you have time you can usually obtain money. But though you have the wealth of a cloakroom attendant at the Canton Hotel, you cannot buy yourself a minute more time than I have, or the cat sitting by the fire has.

IN THE REALM OF TIME, NO
ONE'S RICHER THAN YOU

Philosophers have explained the concept of space. They have not explained time. It is the inexplicable raw material of everything. With it, all is possible; without it, nothing. The supply of time is truly a daily miracle, a genuinely astonishing affair when one examines it. You wake up in the morning, and lo! Your purse is magically filled with 24 hours of the unmanufactured tissue of the universe of your life! It is yours. It is the most precious of possessions, a highly singular commodity, showered upon you in a manner as singular as the commodity itself!

And observe—no one can take it from you. It is not stealable. *And no one receives either more or less than you receive.* Talk about an ideal democracy! In the realm of time there is no aristocracy of wealth, and no aristocracy of intellect. Genius is never rewarded by even an extra hour a day. And there is no punishment for misuse. Waste your infinitely precious commodity as much as you will, and the supply will never be withheld from you. No mysterious power will say: "This is a fool, if not a knave, who does not deserve time, and shall be cut off at the meter." It is more certain than anything, and payment of income is not affected by the length of your working week. Moreover, you cannot draw on your future stores of time. It's impossible to get into debt! You can only waste the passing moment. You cannot waste tomorrow; it is kept for you. You cannot waste the next hour; it is kept for you.

I said the affair was a miracle. Is it not?

AN UNEARNED INCOME OF 24 HOURS A DAY

You have to live on this 24 hours of daily time. Out of it you have to spin health, pleasure, money, contentment, respect and the evolution of your immortal soul. Its right use, its most effective use, is a matter of the highest urgency and of the most thrilling actuality. All depends on that. Your happiness—the elusive prize that you are all clutching for, my friends—depends on that. Strange that the newspapers, so enterprising and up-to-date as they are, are not full of "How to live on a given income of time" instead of "How to live on a given income of money"! Money is far commoner than time. When one reflects, one perceives that money is just about the commonest thing there is. It encumbers the earth in gross heaps.

If one can't contrive to live on a certain income of money, one earns a little more—or steals it, or advertises for it. One doesn't necessarily muddle one's life because one can't quite manage on a thousand pounds a year; one braces the muscles and balances the budget. But if one cannot arrange that an income of 24 hours a day shall exactly cover all proper items of expenditure, one does definitely muddle one's life. The supply of time, though gloriously regular, is cruelly restricted.

WE ALWAYS HAVE ALL THE TIME THERE IS

Which of us lives on 24 hours a day?

And when I say "lives," I do not mean exists or "muddles through." Which of us is free from that uneasy feeling that the "great spending departments" of daily life are not managed as they ought to be? Which of us is quite sure that this fine suit is not surmounted by that shameful hat, or that in paying attention to the china tableware one has forgotten the quality of the food? Which of us is not saying, "I shall alter that when I have a little more time?"

We never shall have any more time. We have, and we have always had, all the time there is. It is the realization of this profound and neglected truth (which, by the way, I have not discovered) that has led me to the minute practical examination of daily time expenditure.

(From *How to Live on 24 Hours a Day* by Arnold Bennett, 1908)

THE IMMENSE, SECRET POWER OF GRATITUDE

Wallace D. Wattles

A grateful mind is a great mind, which eventually attracts to itself great things.

—PLATO

The first step toward getting rich is to convey the idea of your wants to the Divine Substance. This is true, and you will see that in order to do so it becomes necessary to relate yourself to the Divine Intelligence in a harmonious way. The whole process of mental adjustment and atonement can be summed up in one word, *gratitude*.

First, you believe that there is one Intelligent Substance, from which all things proceed; second, you believe that this Substance gives you everything you desire; and third, *you relate yourself to it by a feeling of deep and profound gratitude.*

Many people who order their lives rightly in all other ways are kept in poverty by their lack of gratitude. Having received one gift, they cut the wires that connect them with the Source by failing to make acknowledgment.

GRATITUDE IS THE STATE OF WEALTH

It is easy to understand that the nearer we live to the source of wealth, the more wealth we shall receive. It is also easy to understand that the soul that is always grateful lives in closer touch with the Source than the one who never gives thankful acknowledgment. The more gratefully we fix our minds on the Supreme when good things come to us, the more good things we will receive, and the more rapidly they will come. The reason is simply that the mental attitude of gratitude draws the mind into closer touch with the Source from which the blessings come.

If it is a new thought to you that gratitude brings your whole mind into closer harmony with the creative energies of the universe, consider it well, and you will see that it is true. The good things you already possess have come to you along the line of obedience to certain laws. Gratitude will lead your mind out along the ways by which things come; and it will keep you in close harmony with creative thought and prevent you from falling into competitive thought.

Gratitude alone can keep you looking toward the All, and prevent you from falling into the error of thinking of the supply as limited; to do that would be fatal to your hopes.

There is a Law of Gratitude, and it is absolutely necessary that you should observe the law, if you are to get the results you seek. The Law of Gratitude is the natural principle that action and reaction are always equal, and in opposite directions.

REACH FOR THE DIVINE, AND
THE DIVINE REACHES BACK

The grateful outreaching of your mind in thankful praise to the Supreme is a liberation or expenditure of force. It cannot fail to reach that to which it is addressed, and the reaction is an instantaneous movement toward you. And if your gratitude is strong and constant, the reaction in Divine Substance will be strong and continuous; the movement of the things you want will be always toward you. You cannot exercise much power without gratitude, for it is gratitude that keeps you connected with Power.

But the value of gratitude does not consist solely of getting you more blessings in the future. Without gratitude you cannot long keep from dissatisfied thought regarding things as they are.

The moment you permit your mind to dwell with dissatisfaction upon things as they are, you begin to lose ground. You fix attention upon the common, the ordinary, the poor, and the squalid and mean, and your mind takes the form of these things. Then you will transmit these forms or mental images to the Divine, and the common, the poor, the squalid and mean will come to you.

To permit your mind to dwell upon the inferior is to become inferior and to surround yourself with inferior things. On the other hand, to fix your attention on the best is to surround yourself with the best, and to become the best.

GRATITUDE'S GIFT OF FAITH

The Creative Power within us makes us into the image of that to which we give our attention. We are Thinking Substance, and Thinking Substance always takes the form of that which it thinks about. The grateful mind is constantly fixed upon the best; therefore it tends to become the best. It takes the form or character of the best, and will receive the best.

Also, faith is born of gratitude. The grateful mind continually expects good things, and expectation becomes faith. The reaction of gratitude upon one's own mind produces faith, and every outgoing wave of grateful thanksgiving increases faith. *If you have no feeling of gratitude, you cannot long retain a living faith, and without a living faith you cannot get rich by the creative method*. It is necessary, then, to cultivate the habit of being grateful for every good thing that comes to you and to give thanks continuously. And because all things have contributed to your advancement, you should include all things in your gratitude.

(From *The Science of Getting Rich* by Wallace D. Wattles, 1910)

THE DIVINE USE OF WEALTH

Julia Seton

At one point on the path, our hearts will seek satisfaction through personal selfishness and exaltation of the ego. Personal human desires are bounded more or less by pain, loss, disappointment and the heartbreak of life, but all these form the ladder by which we climb past our dead selves to higher things. All these separate, personal satisfactions are the flowers of the tree of life whose root is *truth*.

The universal use of wealth includes personal satisfaction. It literally means—seek first the kingdom of harmony, and understanding within the self, and all these external things will be added because they come as the result of our powerfully poised, tranquilized consciousness.

In the true use of wealth we can have all our desires expressed to the fullest and live in glad rapture, ministering to the need of others. "The river widens as it nears the sea," and with our own life made powerful, free and unlimited, we can stand as a great revolving light for the darkened minds of the developing multitudes.

We know what wealth really is, why the mind resolutely demands it; knowing the deeper laws of conquest over it, the higher uses of it, we can make our lives become pathways of peace, power and wisdom, over which the whole human race can pass into abundance of supply.

We can give of all we have to those who have not; not "all we have," for that would again beggar us, but *of all* we have, and give without stint, full measure, pressed down and running over.

The New Race mind is turning eagerly to be taught these new lessons. Just as it grasps quickly the new method of conquering its own poverty, just as quickly can it be taught the higher *universal* use of the wealth it has created for itself.

The New Civilization will live life as gods, fashioning their material universe. Thought force rightly directed will build all the energy that creates, into myriad forms of created beauty, harmony and freedom. We are now, and always have been, the creator of our own material universe. We do in truth know we are divine, and can live as an individualized god on our own self-created pathway.

(From *The Key to Health, Wealth and Love* by Julia Seton, 1917)

Part Six

ATTITUDES THAT STAND BETWEEN US AND MONEY

DON'T LIVE IN PROCRASTINATION, LAND OF THE POOR

Napoleon Hill

An accurate analysis of more than 25,000 men and women who had experienced failure disclosed the fact that lack of decision-making took a lead position among 30 major causes of failure. This is no mere statement of a theory—it is a fact.

Procrastination, the opposite of deciding, is a common enemy that practically everybody must conquer. You will have an opportunity to test your capacity to reach quick and definite decisions when you are ready to begin putting into action certain principles.

BE QUICK TO DECIDE, SLOW TO REVISE

An analysis of several hundred people who had accumulated fortunes disclosed the fact that every one of them had the habit of reaching decisions promptly, and of changing these decisions slowly, if and when they were changed. Without exception, people who fail to accumulate money have the habit of reaching decisions, if at all, very slowly, and of changing these decisions quickly and often.

One of Henry Ford's most outstanding qualities was this habit of reaching decisions quickly and definitely, and changing them slowly. This quality was so pronounced in the founder of the American automobile industry that it gave him the reputation of being obstinate. It was this quality that prompted him to continue to manufacture his famous Model T (the world's ugliest car) when all of his advisors, and many of the purchasers of the car, were urging him to change it.

Perhaps Ford delayed too long in making the change, but the other side of the story is that his firmness of decision yielded a huge fortune before the change in model became necessary. There is but little doubt that Ford's habit of definiteness of decision assumed the proportion of obstinacy, but this quality is preferable to slowness in reaching decisions and quickness in changing them.

MAKE SURE YOUR OPINIONS ARE YOUR OWN

Generally, the majority of people who fail to accumulate money sufficient for their needs are also easily influenced by the opinions of others. They permit newspapers and their gossiping neighbors to do their thinking for them, not realizing that opinions are the cheapest commodities on earth. Everyone has a flock of opinions ready to be wished upon anyone who will accept them. If you are influenced by opinions when you reach decisions, you will not succeed in any undertaking, much less in that of transmuting your own desires into money.

If you are influenced by the opinions of others, you will have no desires of your own. Keep your own counsel by reaching your own decisions and following them. Take no one into your confidence, except the members of your "Master Mind" group, and be very sure in your selection of this group that you choose only those who will be in complete sympathy and harmony with your purpose. Close friends and relatives, while not meaning to do so, often handicap one through opinions and sometimes through ridicule, which is meant to be humorous. Thousands of men and women carry inferiority complexes with them all through life because some well-meaning but ignorant person destroyed their confidence through opinions or ridicule.

You have a brain and mind of your own. Use it, and reach your own decisions. If you need facts or information from other people to enable you to reach decisions, as you probably will in many instances, acquire these facts or secure the information you need quietly, without disclosing your purpose.

(From *Think and Grow Rich* by Napoleon Hill, 1937)

PROCRASTINATION:
THE "GOING TO DO IT" TRAP

Julia Seton

The *obsession of tomorrow* spreads out all over those who are caught in its negative dragnet. "Going to do it" is their slogan, "Going to have it" . . . "some day." The future, like a mighty ruler, stands before them and, worshipping it, they are blind, deaf and dumb to their present opportunities.

There are wondrous avenues of accomplishment opening on every hand, but something in their weak consciousness says, "wait," "not now," "some other time." "Going to do it" is the law of procrastination. Procrastination is the seed, and "going to do it" the tree that springs from the obsession.

There is nothing in this world that ever springs spontaneously perfect. Creation, emanation and evolution are cosmic laws, and they are human laws, too. And no matter what we want, have, do or are, we must begin it before we can finish it and possess the fruition. Those who carry hope, dreams and desires hidden in their hearts, and drag through days, months and years without the courage of putting them to the test, must be failures because they are standing ever before their own unfulfilled selfhood. "God helps those who help themselves" has been spoken for centuries, and a thousand unseen forces are waiting to assist those who know what they want and then fling themselves fearlessly in pursuit of their goals.

LOSING THE SUBTLE ESSENCE
OF DIVINE COMMAND

Once I met a great woman, great in genius, great in personality, great in expression. She was training to become a public reader and teacher and perhaps later an actress. In some past incarnations she had fulfilled the law of all these desires and came into life equipped fully for these big endeavors. I was fond of her and eager for the world to have the privilege of enjoying her great gifts. Always she said, "Not yet, but I am going to do it." Then she went on studying, always with this discordant urge within her; she longed to stop and get out into her legitimate field. Whenever she came to me, I said, "Why don't you begin, get ready, announce yourself, get a business manager or get into a company? Won't you please do something to give yourself a chance?" Yes, she would, she was "going to do it." Ten years have passed and she has never done it. Today, after 10 years of foolish resistance and wear and tear on the physical side which repressed genius always brings, she is the decay of a glorious selfhood, lacking that subtle essence of divine command within her own soul. She lost all, and will have to give this incarnation to the development of a consciousness that can direct her own soul. The world is full of those who are "going to do it," and so it is full of failures.

THE WATCHWORD
OF SUCCESS: DO IT NOW

"Do it now" is the watchword of success. Of course it is common sense to give ourselves a legitimate amount of time to get ready for anything. The bigger our endeavor, the more time and thought it demands, and it is well said that "fools rush in where angels fear to tread." It is also true, though, that without this quality in the human soul which causes the fool to rush in, many fools would forever remain at the fool's level of enfoldment. The urge that sends the fool on is the urge that deifies and glorifies our human endeavor. While the fool follows it in uncontrolled, undirected enthusiasm, wise people guide it and cherish it as their most precious possession, training themselves to allow it to urge them on and through almost impossible accomplishments.

"Going to do it" never gets anyone anywhere, and those who rise powerfully to the top of their own mountain of success are those who first survey the path to this mountain pass and then, taking the bit of the bridle of their own lives in their teeth, race to success. It is then that the world, seeing them rush on in what appears to be madness, stops and asks, "What is this?" And with attention comes interest, and through interest comes praise or ridicule, and through these comes cooperation and success is assured. Finding ourselves, knowing what we want to do, giving ourselves a legitimate time for perfecting our ability to do then *doing* it—this is *the law of success.*

Do it now! We may have only one-tenth of one percent perfection when we start anything, but practice makes perfect, and out of the very crudest material will come a gem, polished by use into a resplendent brightness. It is better to do and fail and profit by the wisdom born of this failure, than to sit down in unexpressed genius and atrophy from disuse. "The past is spent, the future is thy God's, today is thine, hold fast the precious treasure."

(From *The Science of Success* by Julia Seton, 1914)

THE DANGER OF DRIFTING
INTO NEGATIVITY

Christian D. Larson

When we analyze the minds of people who have failed, we invariably find that they are either negative, nonconstructive or aimless. Their forces are scattered, and what is in them is seldom applied constructively. There is an emptiness about their personality that indicates negativity. There is an uncertainty in their facial expression that indicates the absence of definite ambition. There is nothing of a positive, determined nature going on in their mental world. They have not taken definite action along any line. They are dependent upon fate and circumstances. They are drifting with some stream and are likely to accomplish little. This does not mean, however, that their mental world is necessarily unproductive; in fact, those very minds are in many instances immensely rich with possibilities. The trouble is, those possibilities continue to be dormant, and what is in them is not being brought forth and trained for definite action or actual results.

In this connection, it is well to remember that negative people and nonconstructive minds never attract that which is helpful in their circumstances. The more you drift, the more people you meet who also drift, while on the other hand, when you begin to make your own life and become positive, you begin to meet more positive people and more constructive circumstances.

This explains why "God helps those who help themselves." When you begin to help yourself, which means to make the best of what is in yourself, you begin to attract to yourself more and more of those helpful things that may exist all about you. In other words, constructive forces attract constructive forces; positive forces attract positive forces.

You thus demonstrate the law that "Nothing succeeds like success" and "To him that hath more shall be given." And here it is well to remember that it is not necessary to possess external things in order to be counted among them "that hath." It is only necessary in the beginning to possess the interior riches; that is to take control of what is in you, and proceed to use it positively with a definite goal in view.

GUARD YOUR INTERIOR TREASURE

They who have control of their own minds have great riches already. They are already successful, and if they continue as they have begun, their success will soon appear in the external world. Thus the wealth that existed at first in the internal only will take shape and form in the external. This is a law that is unfailing, and there is not a man or woman on the face of the earth who cannot apply it with the most satisfying results.

The reason why so many fail is found in the fact that they do not fully and constructively apply the forces and powers they possess, and the reason why so many succeed only to a slight degree is found in the fact that only a small fraction of their power is applied properly.

Sometimes we meet people who have only ordinary ability, but who are very successful. Then we meet others who have great ability but who are not successful, or who succeed only to a slight degree. At first we see no explanation, but when we understand the cause of success as well as the cause of failure, the desired explanation is easily found. If those with ordinary ability comply with the essentials necessary to the right use of mind, they will naturally succeed, though if they had greater ability, their success would of course become greater in proportion. But the individual who has great ability, yet does not apply the essentials necessary to the right use of mind, cannot succeed.

The positive and constructive use of the power of mind, with a definite goal in view, will invariably result in advancement, attainment and achievement, but if we wish to use that power in its full capacity, the action of the mind must be deep. In addition to the right use of the mind, we must also learn the full use of mind, and as the full use implies the use of the whole mind—the deeper mental fields and forces, as well as the usual mental fields and forces—it is necessary to understand the subconscious as well as the conscious.

(From *Your Forces and How to Use Them* by Christian D. Larson, 1912)

FEAR AND WORRY:
THE ENEMIES OF WEALTH

Ralph Waldo Trine

You acquire a particular quality by constantly acting a particular way . . . you become just by performing just actions, temperate by performing temperate actions, brave by performing brave actions.

—ARISTOTLE

It has been said, perhaps over and over again, that we are all, more or less, creatures of habit. Undoubtedly there is much truth in the statement. Both habit-forming and habit-breaking have their origins in purely mental processes, so the question naturally arises—isn't it better to be masters rather than creatures of habit? Especially apt, moreover, is the question when we realize that in every case to be master is by far more profitable, as well as more satisfactory.

It rests upon each one to decide whether he or she will become a master or a creature of circumstances. It depends upon the direction in which we set our faces, and how persistently we then follow the road upon which we set foot. Facing the right direction is the main thing. If, then, we have backbone and stamina and a fair degree of good cheer—which, if pursued persistently, will lead to a merry heart all along the way—there can be but one outcome.

"The key to every man," said Emerson, "is his thought—sturdy and defiant though he look, he has a helm which he obeys, which is the idea after which all his facts are classified." Whichever way we look, we will find that thought is at the bottom of all progress or retrogression, of all that is desirable or undesirable in human life. As within, so without, it is simply a matter of sequence—it follows the elemental law of cause and effect.

FEAR IS NOT NATURAL

That we have the power to determine what types of thought we entertain and live with is one of the tremendous facts of human life—it is the great determining factor. It was that able writer who dealt with the mind's processes in their relation to life, James Allen, who said: "A man can only rise, conquer, and achieve by lifting up his thoughts. He can only remain weak and abject and miserable by refusing to live up to his thoughts . . . Action is the blossom of thought, and joy and suffering are its fruits; thus does a man garner in the sweet and bitter fruitage of his own husbandry."

There are certain types of thoughts and emotions that may be called the natural, the normal, the God-intended, since there follows in their train only good. Among these are hope, faith, courage, good cheer, love, sympathy, forgiveness, joy and peace. They are positive and uplifting and body-building. They seem to act upon the life forces within so as to stimulate, or even to restore and to maintain, harmony. They stimulate the circulation and the processes of nutrition. They make both for mental and bodily health and strength and vigor.

Again there are types of thoughts and emotions that seem to be perversions, the unnatural and abnormal. Among these are fear, worry, long-continued grief, anger, hatred, avarice. All these might be termed either negative or low types of thoughts and emotions. They produce disturbance and generate weakness in both mind and body. They lead to retrogression rather than to growth. Some of them work through a slow, corroding, pulling-down process; while others are more quick-acting in their poisoning, destructive influences.

COMMANDING FIGURES
DO NOT FEAR

There are probably no influences that cause greater loss and produce more havoc in the individual life than the two closely allied habits of fear and worry. It is difficult to deal with them apart, so nearly related are they.

First in regard to fear. We find it everywhere—fear that what is ours today may not be ours tomorrow, fear for the loss of position or possession or friends, fear of accident, fear of disease, fear of death—or if not ourselves, fear that something will befall this one or that one near or dear to us. We fear while inside—that something may happen, though we do not know what. When out on God's broad highway we fear that the bogeyman, in whatever form he may take in any particular life, will stalk across our path.

We must take ourselves out of the class of the "afraid," the abnormal. *The commanding figures in life do not fear.* The others, who are giving time to fear, are allowing the neutralizing and even paralyzing power of this perverted mental force to work its havoc in their lives. They are giving time, then, to seeing the ideal they would actualize or attain to, and are then setting into activity strong, definite types of thought-forces that are hourly and even instantly working for them along the negative lines they are going.

FEAR: A SORT OF PUBLIC DRUNKENNESS

Fear and worry steal the effectiveness from human endeavor and happiness. To reach the point where we in time become free from them is, after all, a matter of self-control. Others lack this control in other things, and they pay their heavy tolls. Drunkards lack this self-control when it comes to a too frequent companionship with the bottle. They pay the price, and many times they would give the world to get from under the grip of the habit. Society then casts its stigma upon them, and they pay the price double-fold. The time, I believe, is coming when he or she who lacks self-control when it comes to these senseless and useless—worse than useless—habits of fear and worry will have to bear the same stigma that others who lack self-control along other lines are compelled to bear today.

"It's so natural for me to worry," says one, "and I can't help it." The first part of the statement may be true in many cases. "Nonsense!" should be the reply always to the latter part of it. If you think you can't help it, and if you persist in this thought, the chances are that you can't, and there is perhaps then no hope for you. But take the other thought— take the thought that you can help it; realize once and for all that you can and determine that you will, and if you keep your mind true to that idea and to that purpose, it is simply a matter of time until you will have taken yourself entirely out of the class of the "afraid," the "get-nowhere."

We habitually concern ourselves with so many things that we really need not concern ourselves with. We concern ourselves with so many small matters of mere detail, instead of concerning ourselves primarily with the fundamentals, and allowing the matters of detail to fall in place naturally and of their own accord. The one given to fear or worry concerns himself or herself with a hundred things every day, and some even every night, that there is not the slightest reason for concerning oneself with at all. In a simple, homely way, John Vance Cheney put a great truth along this line when he said:

> The happiest heart that ever beat
> Was in some quiet breast,
> That found the common daylight sweet,
> And left to Heaven the rest.

THE TWO THINGS NEVER TO WORRY ABOUT

"There are two things," says a thoughtful writer, "which will make us happy in this life, if we attend to them. The first is, never to vex ourselves about what we cannot help; and the second, never to vex ourselves about what we can help." Happiness always keeps considerably ahead of the one who is given to the habit of either fear or worry. Such a one seems also to have the faculty of helping, at least, to keep it away from others.

We all have our weak points; for anything approaching an ideal growth and development and thereby attainment, we must, as we sometimes say, call ourselves up specifically now and then. We get so accustomed to running in ruts that we can never hope for anything other than a limited or a one-sided development, unless we do this occasionally. We must remember that by fear and worry nothing is ever to be gained, but much is always to be lost. By this negative attitude of mind, we open the doors, many times, for the entrance of the very conditions we fear may come upon us.

When the fear becomes sufficiently deep-seated, we many times invite what we fear, just as, by a different attitude of mind, we invite and attract the influences and conditions we desire. Subtle, but always working and all-powerful, are the operations of the thoughts and the emotions, and it is here that we must look for the bulk of whatever comes into our lives. A deep psychological law was undoubtedly at work in the life of him who said: "For the thing which I greatly feared is come upon me, and that which I was afraid of is come unto me."

It would seem almost better that a certain percentage of the things we worry about do come upon us or come about—so that they do their worst and be done with it, as we say—rather than that we remain continual slaves to the hosts of things that we fear may come and that we ceaselessly worry about. But the interesting part is that hardly any of these things ever do come. Even remembering this fact does not seem to be able to teach us the folly and the utter uselessness of these habits. How many bridges do we mentally cross that we eventually find we really never do have to cross at all!

We would not only be surprised, but astounded, if we really knew the number of people who have grown habitually timid in their minds and spirits, and whose bodies have been reduced to a low and sluggish tone through the influences we are addressing. The number of people living way below par, mentally and physically, as an effect of fear and worry is simply enormous. In addition to this general lowering of practically all bodily functions and powers, in thousands of cases fear and worry focus their effects on specific ailments and diseases, according to the particular weaknesses of the individual in whose life they gain a foothold. The law of correspondence is wonderfully exact in its workings.

We are what we repeatedly do.

—ARISTOTLE

(From *The New Alignment of Life* by Ralph Waldo Trine, 1918)

NEVER FEAR, DESPITE AN EMPTY PURSE

Julia Seton

The thing we fear always comes upon us; fear is just as direct a line of relationship as love; it is not the amount we spend that counts, but the way in which we spend it.

When we can spend our last dollar knowing, internally, that it is impossible for us to become penniless, we then get a position which will not only let that dollar go, but will bring us another over the same line of transference.

When we are alone in a strange city and look into our wallet and find not a penny, the way to keep it empty is to recognize this lack and become paralyzed with fear and anxiety for the morrow.

Most people do this without knowing the laws they are setting into motion. Their very recognition establishes their relationship with the things they do not want. When we teach ourselves to look into an empty purse with the same feeling of opulence that we should have if we saw a thousand dollars in it, then we have laid hold of the energy that creates, and no power on earth can prevail to keep that purse empty. It is not in the doing but in the "being opulent" that we get the power. We must know how to look behind the things created (notes and coins) into the energy that creates, and this recognition held steadfastly brings life into relation with higher lines of attraction.

(From *The Key to Health, Wealth and Love* by Julia Seton, 1917)

SELF-PITY PUSHES WEALTH AWAY

James Allen

D o not complain that the rich oppress you. Are you sure that if you gained riches you would not be an oppressor yourself? Remember that there is the eternal law which is absolutely just, and that those who oppress today must themselves be oppressed tomorrow; and from this there is no way of escape. And perhaps yesterday you were rich and an oppressor, and now you are merely paying off the debt that you owe to the great law. Practice, therefore, fortitude and faith, and dwell constantly upon the eternal justice, the eternal good.

Endeavor to lift yourself above the personal and the transitory into the impersonal and permanent. Shake off the delusion that you are being injured or oppressed by another. Try to realize, by a more profound comprehension of your inner life and the laws that govern that life, that *you are only really injured by what is within you*.

There is no practice more degrading, debasing and soul-destroying than that of self-pity. Cast it out from you. While such a canker is feeding upon your heart, you can never expect to grow into a fuller life. Cease from the condemnation of others. Instead, condone none of your acts, desires or thoughts that will not bear comparison with spotless purity, or endure the light of sinless good. By so doing you will be building your house upon the rock of the Eternal, and all that is required for your happiness and well-being will come to you in its own time.

There is positively no way of permanently rising above poverty, or any undesirable condition, except by eradicating those selfish and negative conditions within, of which these are the reflection, and by virtue of which they continue. The way to true riches is to enrich the soul by the acquisition of virtue. Outside of real heart-virtue there is neither prosperity nor power, but only the appearances of these.

I am aware that people make money who have acquired no measure of virtue, and have little desire for virtue; but such money does not constitute true riches, and its possession is transitory and feverish. The prosperity of the wicked was a great trial to King David until he went into the sanctuary of God, and then he knew their end. You likewise may go into that sanctuary. It is within you. It is that state of consciousness that remains when all that is sordid, personal and impermanent is risen above, and universal and eternal principles are realized.

THE VIRTUELESS RICH ARE
REALLY THE POOR

That is the God state of consciousness; it is the Sanctuary of the Most High. When by long strife and self-discipline, you have succeeded in entering the door of that holy temple, you will perceive, with unobstructed vision, the end and fruit of all human thought and endeavor, both good and evil. You will then no longer relax your faith when you see immoral people accumulating outward riches, for you will know that they must come again to poverty and degradation.

Rich people who are barren of virtue are, in reality, poor, and as surely as the waters of the river are drifting to the ocean, so surely is he, in the midst of all his riches, drifting toward poverty and misfortune; and though they die rich, yet must they return to reap the bitter fruit of all of their immorality. And though they become rich many times, yet as many times must they be thrown back into poverty, until, by long experience and suffering, they conquer the poverty within. But those who are outwardly poor, yet rich in virtue, are truly rich, and in the midst of all their poverty they are surely traveling toward prosperity, and abounding joy and bliss await their coming.

If you would become truly and permanently prosperous, you must first become virtuous. It is therefore unwise to aim directly at prosperity, to make it the one object of life, to reach out greedily for it. To do this is to ultimately defeat yourself. Rather, aim at self-perfection; make useful and unselfish service the object of your life, and ever reach out hands of faith toward the supreme and unalterable Good.

WEALTH IS DRAWN TO A GOOD STEWARD

You say you desire wealth, not for your own sake, but in order to do good with it, and to bless others. If this is your real motive in desiring wealth, then wealth will come to you; for you are strong and unselfish indeed if, in the midst of riches, you are willing to look upon yourself as steward and not as owner. But examine well your motive, for in the majority of instances where money is desired for the admitted object of blessing others, the real underlying motive is a love of popularity, and a desire to pose as a philanthropist or reformer. If you are not doing good with what little you have, depend upon it that the more money you acquire the more selfish you will become, and all the good you appear to do with your money, if you attempt to do any, will be self-aggrandizement.

If your real desire is to do good, there is no need to wait for money before you do it; you can do it now, this very moment, and just where you are. If you are really so unselfish as you believe yourself to be, you will show it by sacrificing yourself for others now. No matter how poor you are, there is room for self-sacrifice. The heart that truly desires to do good does not wait for money before doing it, but comes to the altar of sacrifice, and, leaving there the unworthy elements of self, goes out and breathes the breath of blessings upon neighbor and stranger.

As the effect is related to the cause, so are prosperity and power related to the inward good, and poverty and weakness to the inward evil. Money does not constitute true wealth, or position, or power, and to rely upon it alone is to stand upon a slippery place.

Power Is Released by Freedom from Poverty

Your true wealth is your stock of virtue, and your true power the uses to which you put it. Rectify your heart and you will rectify your life. Lust, hatred, anger, vanity, pride, covetousness, self-indulgence, self-seeking, obstinacy— all these are poverty and weakness; whereas love, purity, gentleness, meekness, patience, compassion, generosity, self-forgetfulness and self-renunciation—all these are wealth and power.

As the elements of poverty and weakness are overcome, an irresistible and all-conquering power is evolved from within, and those who succeed in establishing themselves in the highest virtue bring the whole world to their feet. But the rich, as well as the poor, have their undesirable conditions, and are frequently further removed from happiness than the poor. And here we see how happiness depends not upon outward aids or possessions but upon the inward life.

Come, then, out of your poverty; come out of your pain; come out of your troubles, heartaches and loneliness by coming out of yourself. Let the old tattered garment of your petty self-centeredness fall from you, and put on the new garment of universal love. You will then realize the inward heaven, and it will be reflected in all your outward life.

Those who set their feet firmly upon the path of self-conquest, who walk aided by the staff of faith on the highway of self-sacrifice, will assuredly achieve the highest prosperity, and will reap abounding and enduring joy and bliss.

(From *As a Man Thinketh* by James Allen, 1903)

ARE YOU FILLING OUT
YOUR OWN PINK SLIP?

Joseph Murphy

If you are working in a large organization and you are silently thinking of and resenting the fact that you are underpaid, that you are not appreciated, and that you deserve more money and greater recognition, you are subconsciously severing your ties with that organization. You are setting a law in motion, and the superintendent or manager will say to you, "We have to let you go." *Actually, you dismissed yourself.* The manager was simply the instrument through which your own negative mental state was confirmed. It was an example of the law of action and reaction. The action was your thought, and the reaction was the response of your subconscious mind.

(From *The Power of Your Subconscious Mind* by Joseph Murphy, 1963)

THE PENNY-PINCHING ARE NEVER RICH

Julia Seton

No life can reach this plane of seeing and feeling opulent, and creating an opulent atmosphere, by allowing itself to go in old-thought ruts where everything speaks to it of poverty and under-supply.

We cannot create wealth by pinching our earnings and holding on in fear to the thing we have. If we have only a dollar, and must spend it, we must learn to let it go as if we had a thousand behind it (for we really have when we know the truth of divine supply and consciously unite ourselves with it). When we do not have this interior consciousness and try to spend our last cent, and instead of being opulent we have the hearts of cowards and beggars, we had better hold on to it, for no more dollars will come when we send it over such lines of connection.

COUNTING ON COMPETITION
INSTEAD OF DIVINE SUPPLY

There are two avenues of transference to every life; one is the plane of competition and the other the plane of divine transference.

We who come into the abundance of supply come under the laws of the plane of divine transference and our banker is universal mind; those who recognize lack and limited supply are on the plane of competition and their bankers are people often as limited as themselves. On the latter plane, this power of seeing opulently is as exact a law as on the plane of divine transference. Abundance of supply on the competitive plane is spasmodic; one is rich this year and poor the next; there is no peace or power of possession; but under the Law of Divine Transference we get, we have and we hold forever.

The plane of competition is the everyday world of cause and effect, and the working out of getting and taking from ourselves and others. The plane of divine transference is the one of universal recognition of supply, and the working out of our own and another's rights on the plane of receiving and giving. On these higher spiritual and intellectual planes of consciousness, the lines never cross nor tangle, but each one runs directly home to the center of self; and over the same line on which we send out our inspired desires, there passes back to us the answer to our prayers.

The plane of competition is where the majority of us are working. They are under the law of get and take, an eye for an eye, a tooth for a tooth. There are lives everywhere working under the old law of the plane of competition and sighing for the results which only the Law of Divine Transference can give. They are like the chickens in this familiar story.

A woman who had a great love for poultry decided that she would go into the chicken business, so she rented a small piece of land and gave up her time to the production of the finest possible breed of hens. During her years with the fowls she gained a great deal of practical, even meta-physical knowledge. In relating some of her many observa-tions and experiences she said: "Chickens are just like human beings, they have the same desires and they make the same mistakes and suffer from the reaction of their ignorance just as we do. I never feed the chickens, but I find something to use as a lesson for myself.

"Whenever it is time to feed them, I take a huge pan full of many good things which chickens like and, placing it in the center of the yard, call them. Some of them are near, some of them are far away, but at the sound of my voice and call, they all come running pell-mell. Some of the hens which are nearest the pan grab a mouthful out of it and run away toward the corner of the yard. Others, seeing them with a piece of food in their mouths, chase wildly after them, totally ignoring my call and the full pan of food just before them.

"Before many minutes all the hens are out in the farthest corners, away from the food, fighting, scrambling and tum-bling over each other in their attempts to secure the morsel which was in the mouths of the few, entirely unconscious of the big full pan of supply waiting just within easy reach.

"Isn't this the way with humans? Someone gets a little

supply out of the great universal pan, and then the blind beside them begin to struggle with them to get possession of their little bit without going straight to the universal source itself which is always waiting, full and free for them to come and take. The universal good awaits our return with the same natural law that awaited the hens.

"When the hens got through struggling and no one had anything, the pan was still standing waiting to supply in full the hunger and wants of those who found their way back. I have to call them back many times before they satisfy themselves from the pan and not from the bits they wrested from each other."

(From *The Science of Success* by Julia Seton, 1914)

Part Seven

A RICH
INNER LIFE IS SOON
RICH OUTSIDE

INTUITION: OUR LINK TO THE SOURCE OF ALL RICHES

Ralph Waldo Trine

Intuition is to the spiritual nature and understanding what sense perception is to the sensuous nature and understanding. It is an inner spiritual sense through which we are opened to the direct revelation and knowledge of the secrets of nature and life. Through intuition we are brought into conscious unity and fellowship with the Source, and made to realize our own deific nature and supremacy of being. Spiritual supremacy and illumination, thus realized through the development and perfection of intuition under divine inspiration, gives the perfect inner vision and direct insight into the character, properties and purpose of all things to which the attention and interest are directed.

It is, we repeat, a spiritual sense opening inwardly, as the physical senses open outwardly. Because it has the capacity to perceive, grasp and know the truth at firsthand, independent of all external sources of information, we call it intuition. All inspired teaching and spiritual revelations are based upon the recognition of this spiritual faculty of the soul, and its power to receive and appropriate them.

Conscious unity in spirit and purpose with the Source, born out of supreme desire and trust, opens the soul through this inner sense. Then come immediate inspiration and enlightenment from the Divine Omniscience, and the cooperative energy of the Divine Omnipotence, under which there is created a seer and a master.

On this higher plane of realized spiritual life in the flesh, the mind holds an impersonal attitude and acts with unfettered freedom and unbiased vision, grasping truth at firsthand, independent of all external sources of information. Approaching all beings and things from the divine side, they are seen in the light of the Divine Omniscience. God's purpose in them, and so the truth concerning them, as it rests in the mind of God, are revealed by direct illumination from the Divine Mind, to which the soul is opened inwardly through this spiritual sense we call intuition. Some call it the voice of the soul; some call it the voice of God; some call it the sixth sense. It is our inner spiritual sense.

To the degree that we come into the recognition of our own true selves, into the realization of the oneness of our life with the Infinite Life, and to the degree that we open ourselves to this divine inflow, does this voice of intuition, this voice of the soul, this voice of God, speak clearly. In the degree that we recognize, listen to and obey it, does it speak ever more clearly, until by-and-by there comes the time when it is unerring, absolutely unerring, in its guidance.

(From *In Tune with the Infinite* by Ralph Waldo Trine, 1897)

"THAT CALM CONFIDENCE THAT COMMANDS SUCCESS": ANOTHER VIEW OF INTUITION

James Allen

As you succeed in gaining mastery over your impulses and thoughts, you will begin to feel, growing up within you, a new and silent power, and a settled feeling of composure and strength will remain with you. Your latent powers will begin to unfold themselves, and whereas your efforts were formerly weak and ineffectual, you will now be able to work with that calm confidence that commands success. Along with this new power and strength, there will be awakened within you that interior illumination known as "intuition," and you will walk no longer in darkness and speculation, but in light and certainty. With the development of this soul-vision, judgment and mental penetration will be incalculably increased, and there will evolve within you that prophetic vision by the aid of which you will be able to sense coming events and to forecast, with remarkable accuracy, the result of your efforts.

And in just the measure that you alter from within, will your outlook upon life alter. As you alter your mental attitude toward others they will alter in their attitude and conduct toward you. As you rise above the lower, debilitating and destructive thought-forces, you will come in contact with the positive, strengthening and up-building currents generated by strong, pure and noble minds; your happiness will be immeasurably intensified, and you will begin to realize the joy, strength and power born only of self-mastery. This joy, strength and power will be continually radiating from you. Without any effort on your part, though you are utterly unconscious of it, strong people will be drawn toward you, influence will be put into your hands, and outward events will shape themselves in accordance with your altered thought-world.

(From *From Poverty to Power, or the Realization of Prosperity and Peace* by James Allen, 1906)

VISUALIZATION: TURNING THE MIND INTO A MAGNET

Orison S. Marden

There is a power that is creative, that operates everywhere; a power that is destined to lift every created thing up to the peak of its possibilities. This power is latent in you, awaiting expression, awaiting your cooperation to realize your ambition. The first step toward utilizing it is to visualize the ideal of what you want to make real, the ideal of the man or the woman you aim to be, and the things you want to do. Without this initial step the further process of creating is impossible.

Great discoverers, scientists, explorers, philanthropists, inventors, philosophers, who have pushed the world forward and done immeasurable service for humanity—such as Columbus, Goodyear, Fulton, Edison, Bell—have visualized their dreams. They have nursed their visions through long years, many of them in the midst of poverty, persecution, ridicule and opposition of all sorts, until they brought their dreams to earth and made them realities.

In making a study of the methods of successful men and women, I have found that they are almost invariably strong and vivid visualizers of the things they are trying to accomplish. They are intense workers as well as dreamers, and nurse their vision tenaciously until they match it with reality. They build castles in the air, but they put the solid foundation of reality under them.

One of the most illustrious opera singers of our past was a poor girl singing in the little church choir in her native village in Maine. When even her own people thought it a disgrace for a girl to appear on the stage, to sing in public concerts or in opera, she was picturing herself a great prima donna singing before vast audiences in the United States, in foreign capitals, and before the crowned heads of Europe.

FROM THE BARNYARD AND THE PUSHCART TO THE HALLS OF FAME

Young Henry Clay practiced oratory before the domestic animals in a Virginia barn and barnyard, visualizing himself swaying vast audiences by his eloquence.

When Washington was a lad of 12 he pictured himself as a leader, rich and powerful, a man of vast importance in the life of the colonies, and the ruler of a nation he would help to create.

When the young John Wanamaker was delivering clothing from a pushcart in Philadelphia, he saw himself as the proprietor of a much larger establishment than any that existed in that city. He saw beyond that and glimpsed the

Wanamaker of later days, the great powerful merchant, operating immense stores in the world's leading capitals.

Young Andrew Carnegie pictured himself a powerful figure in the steel world.

Now this sort of visualizing is not mere vanity or petty egotism. *It is the God urge in individuals* pushing them out beyond themselves, beyond what is visible to the physical eye, to better things. The Scriptures tell us that "without a vision the people perish." I have never known anyone to do anything out of the ordinary who was never able to see beyond the visible into the vast invisible universe containing the things that might be; who did not keep clearly in mind the vision of the particular thing he or she was trying to accomplish.

TO SEE THE UNSEEN IS
TO MAKE IT REAL

It is the person who can visualize what does not yet exist in the visible world about us and see it as a reality; who can see opportunities where others see no chance; who sees power, opulence, plenty and success where others see only failure, limitation, poverty and wretchedness, who eventually pushes to the top and wins out.

Many people seem to think that the imagination, or visualizing faculty, is not a fundamental or necessary part of the brain, and they have never taken it very seriously. But those of us who have studied mental laws know that it is one of the most important functions of the mind. We are beginning to discover that the power to visualize is a sort of advance courier, making announcement of the things that the Creator has qualified us to bring about. In other words, we are beginning to see that our visions are prophecies of our future: mental movies of what we are supposed to carry out, to make a concrete reality.

For instance, a young person whose leaning is entirely in another direction is not haunted by an architectural vision, an art vision, a merchandising vision or a vision of some other calling for which he or she has no natural affinity. A girl does not dream of a musical career for years before she has the slightest opportunity for taking up music as a career if she has no musical talent, or if her ability along other lines is much more pronounced. Boys and girls, men and women, are not haunted by dreams telling them to do what nature has not fitted them for. We dream a particular dream, see a particular vision, because we have the talent and the special ability to bring the dream, the vision, into reality.

THERE'S DIVINITY BEHIND
OUR VISIONS

Of course, I do not mean by dreams and visions the mere fantasies, the vague, undefined thoughts that flit through the mind, but our real heart longings, our soul yearnings, the mental pictures of a future that haunts our dreams, and the insistent urge which prods us until we try to match them with their reality, to bring them out into the actual. There is a divinity behind these visions. They are prophecies of our possible future, and nature is throwing up these pictures on our mental screen to give us a glimpse of the possibilities that are awaiting us.

One reason why most of us do such little, unoriginal things is because we do not sufficiently nurse our visions and longings. The plan of the building must come before the building. We climb by the ladder of our visions, our dreams. The sculptor's model must live in the sculptor's mind before it can be called out of the marble. We do not fully realize the mental force we generate by persistently visualizing our ideal, by the perpetual clinging to our dreams, the vision of the thing we long to do or to be. We do not know that nursing our desires makes the mental pictures sharper, more clean-cut, and that these mental processes are completing the plans of our future life building, filling in the outlines and details, and drawing to us out of the invisible energy of the universe the materials for our actual building.

MAKING A MAGNET OF THE MIND

There is no other one thing you will find so helpful in the attainment of your ambition as the habit of visualizing what you are trying to accomplish, visualizing it vividly, just as distinctly, just as vigorously as possible, because this makes a magnet of the mind to attract what one is after. All about us we see individuals focusing their minds with intensity and persistence on their special aims and attracting to themselves marvelous results.

Even if you are only a humble employee—a stock clerk, an office assistant, a cook—visualize yourself as the person you long to be, see yourself in the exalted position you long to attain. *There is nothing more potent in drawing your heart's desire to you than visualizing that desire*, dreaming your dream, seeing yourself as the ideal of your vision, filling the position in which your ambition would place you.

No matter what happens, always hold fast to the thought that you can be what you long to be, that you can do the thing you want to do, and picture yourself always as succeeding in what you desire to come true in your life. Do this no matter how many urgent duties or obligations may for a time hold you back, how many circumstances and conditions may seem to contradict the possibility of your success. Do this no matter how many people, even your own people, may blame or misunderstand you, may even call you a crank, crazy, a conceited egotist; hold fast to your faith in your dream, in yourself.

Cling to your vision. Nurse it, for it is the God-inspired model by which you are being urged to shape your life.

Do these things and work with all your might for the attainment of your goal on the physical plane, and *nothing* can hinder your success.

(From *The Key to Prosperity: Conquering Poverty Thinking* by Orison S. Marden, edited by David Morgan, 2004)

SEE IT FIRST, THEN BE IT

Joseph Murphy

Many years ago I met a young boy in Australia who wanted to become a physician and surgeon but he had no money. I explained to him how a seed deposited in the soil attracts to itself everything necessary for its unfolding, and that all he had to do was to take a lesson from the seed and deposit the required idea in his subconscious mind. To earn some money this young, brilliant boy used to clean out doctors' offices, wash windows and do odd repair jobs. He told me that every night, as he went to sleep, he used to picture in his mind's eye a medical diploma on a wall with his name on it in big, bold letters. He used to clean and shine the framed diplomas in the medical building where he worked. It was not hard for him to engrave the image of a diploma in his mind and develop it there. Definite results followed as he persisted with his mental picture every night for about four months.

The sequel of this story was very interesting. One of the doctors took a great liking to this young boy and, after training him in the art of sterilizing instruments, giving hypodermic injections and other miscellaneous first-aid work, he employed him as a technical assistant in his office. The doctor later sent him to medical school at his own expense. Today, this young man is a prominent medical doctor in Montreal. He discovered the law of attraction by using his subconscious mind the right way. He operated an age-old law that says, "*Having seen the end, you have willed the means to the realization of the end.*" The end in this case was to become a medical doctor.

MAKE IT REAL AND IT SOON WILL BE

This young man was able to imagine, see and feel the reality of being a doctor. He lived with that idea, sustained it, nourished it and loved it until through his imagination it penetrated the layers of his subconscious mind and became a conviction, thereby attracting to him everything necessary for the fulfillment of his dream.

(From *The Power of Your Subconscious Mind* by Joseph Murphy, 1963)

SEE IT, DESPITE OLD THOUGHTS CREEPING IN

Julia Seton

Creation in consciousness comes slowly at first, for the ordinary mind has not been taught to hold a perfect vision. The old distorted visions of the lesser thinking will intrude again and again; negative forms must be displaced by the perfected form with which we wish to be surrounded.

There is not an hour in our lives when we are acting without a vision. We are always creating either the thing we want or the thing we do not want, and the New Civilization realizes the folly of creating for itself pictures of the things it does not want, which, when they appear, can only bind it closer into limitations.

There are some minds that are full of negative images. Their whole field of consciousness is lined with distorted thought-forms of poverty and bad luck: shanties, hovels, misfortune, doubt and fear. These have been their daily projections and they have vitalized them until they materialized.

After we begin to create in consciousness, some of our thought images will be crude, but so are an artist's first pictures crude, but to those who really see the vision and feel the law, there is no turning back and there can be no such word as failure. Standing fast in an unfaltering faith, with the vision perfect in consciousness, anyone can drive the new creation straight through their old environment. Holding it there, the atomic mind of substance cannot refuse to produce it around us in form.

Plenty of whatever we project, or make believe, must come out into form; our realization becomes actualization and we are then in our law of divine transference, which no one can limit but ourselves.

(From *Concentration: The Secret of Success* by Julia Seton, 1916)

HAVE FAITH IN FAITH

Christian D. Larson

We are twice armed if we fight with faith.

—PLATO

To promote the highest development and the most thorough use of character and ability, faith becomes indispensable. Faith awakens everything within us that is superior, and brings out the best that is within. Faith unites us with the Infinite, and no one of us can accomplish the great things in life unless we work constantly in oneness with the Infinite. No mind can do much without the Supreme, and we cannot do our best in any sphere of action unless we live so near to the Supreme that the divine presence is consciously felt at all times.

We are helped by a higher power, and we can receive far greater and superior assistance from this same source when our faith is high and strong. A highly developed mind may accomplish much without faith, but with faith that same mind can accomplish a great deal more, and the same is true of every mind in every stage of development. Faith increases the power, the capacity and the efficiency of everything and everybody.

One of the greatest essentials to the mastery of fate is to have a high goal, a definite goal, and to keep the eye single upon this goal. And there is nothing that causes the mind to aim as high as faith.

FAITH DENIES LIMITS BY PASSING THEM

Faith goes out upon the boundlessness of all things; it passes by the borderland and proves there is no borderland. It demonstrates conclusively that all things are possible and that there is no end to the path of attainment; and what is more, it demonstrates that this path to greater and greater attainment is substantial and sound all the way. There is no seeming void; all is solid rock; therefore it is perfectly safe to go out anywhere into the universal. In the eyes of faith, there is no gulf between the small and the great; from the smaller to the greater there is a path of smooth and solid rock, and anyone may safely reach the greater by simply pressing on.

To master fate, the mind must be determined to reach the highest goal in view, and should realize that the goal can be reached—that it is being reached. And there is nothing that makes the mind more determined to reach the heights than a strong, living faith. Faith sees the heights; faith knows they are there, and can be reached. Therefore, to a mind that would create a grander fate, nothing is more valuable than faith.

FAITH IS NOT BELIEF

To attain faith we must understand that it is not blind belief; *it is not belief at all.* Faith is a live conviction, illumined knowledge received at firsthand through the awakening of that power within that sees, knows and understands the spirit of things.

Consequently, faith not only awakens higher and mightier powers, and illumines the mind with light, wisdom and truth of incalculable value. It also brings mind into perfect touch with those laws and principles that lie at the very foundation of all life, all attainment, all achievement and all change; and it is these laws that mind must employ if fate is to be mastered, and a greater destiny created.

To attain faith, have faith; have faith in the Supreme; have faith in your fellows; have faith in yourself; have faith in everything in the universe, and above all, *have faith in faith*.

(From *Mastery of Fate* by Christian D. Larson, 1910)

YOUR ONLY BUSINESS IS BELIEF

Robert Collier

To begin with, all wealth depends upon a clear understanding of the fact that mind—thought— is the only creator. The great business of life is thinking. Control your thoughts and you control circumstance. Just as the first law of gain is desire, so the formula of success is **BELIEF**. Believe that you have it—see it as an existent fact—and anything you can rightly wish for is yours. Belief is "the substance of things hoped for, the evidence of things not seen." You have seen men, inwardly no more capable than yourself, accomplish the seemingly impossible. You have seen others, after years of hopeless struggle, suddenly win their most cherished dreams. And you've often wondered, "What is the power that gives new life to their dying ambitions, that supplies new impetus to their jaded desires and gives them a new start on the road to success?" That power is belief, faith. Someone, something, gave them a new belief in themselves and a new faith in their power to win—and they leaped ahead and wrested success from seemingly certain defeat.

. . . It is your own belief in yourself that counts. It is the consciousness of dominant power within you that makes all things attainable. You can do anything you think you can. This knowledge is literally the gift of the gods, for through it you can solve every human problem. It should make of you an incurable optimist. It is the open door to welfare. Keep it open—by expecting to gain everything that is right. You are entitled to every good thing. Therefore expect nothing but good. Defeat does not need to follow victory. You don't have to "touch wood" every time you congratulate yourself that things have been going well with you. Victory should follow victory—and it will if you "let this mind be in you which was also in Christ Jesus." It is the mind that means health and life and boundless opportunity and recompense. No limitation rests upon you, so don't let any enter your life. Remember that Mind will do every good thing for you. It will remove mountains for you. "Bring ye all the tithes into the storehouse, and prove me now herewith," saith the Lord of hosts, "if I will not open you the windows of heaven, and pour you out a blessing, that there shall not be room enough to receive it."

Bring all your thoughts, your desires, your aims, your talents into the Storehouse—the Consciousness of Good, the Law of Infinite supplies—and prove these blessings. There is every reason to know that you are entitled to adequate provision. Everything that is involved in supply is a thing of thought. Now reach out, stretch your mind and try to comprehend unlimited thought, unlimited supply. Do not think that supply must come through one or two channels. It is not for you to dictate to Universal Mind the means through which It shall send Its gifts to you. There are millions of channels through which It can reach you. Your part is to impress upon Mind your need, your earnest desire, your boundless belief in the resources and the willingness of Universal Mind to help you. Plant the seed of desire. Nourish it with a clear visualization of the ripened fruit. Water it with sincere faith. But leave the means to Universal Mind. Open up your mind. Clear out the channels of thought. Keep yourself in a state of receptivity. Gain a mental attitude in which you are constantly expecting good. You have the fundamental right to all good, you know. "According to your faith, be it unto you."

The trouble with most of us is that we are mentally lazy.

It is much easier to go along with the crowd than to break trail for ourselves. But the great discoverers, the great inventors, the great geniuses in all lines have been men and women who dared to break with tradition, who defied precedent, who believed that there is no limit to what Mind can do—and who stuck to that belief until their goal was won, in spite of all the sneers and ridicule of the wiseacres and those who said, "It can't be done." Not only that, but they were never satisfied with achieving just one success. They knew that the first success is like the first olive out of the bottle. All the others come out the more easily for it. They realized that they were a part of the Creative Intelligence of the Universe, and that the part shares all the properties of the whole. And that realization gave them the faith to strive for any right thing, the knowledge that the only limit upon their capabilities was the limit of their desires. Knowing that, they couldn't be satisfied with any ordinary success. They had to keep on and on and on.

Edison didn't sit down and fold his hands when he gave us the talking machine or the electric light. These great achievements merely opened the way to new fields of accomplishment. Open up the channels between your mind and Universal Mind, and there is no limit to the riches that will come pouring in. Concentrate your thoughts on the particular thing you are most interested in and ideas in abundance will come flooding down, opening up a dozen ways of winning the goal you are striving for. But don't let one success—no matter how great—satisfy you. The Law of Creation, you know, is the Law of Growth. You can't stand still. You must go forward—or be passed by. Complacency—self-satisfaction—is the greatest enemy of achievement. You must keep looking forward. Like Alexander, you must be constantly seeking new worlds to conquer. Depend upon it—the power will come to meet the need. There is no such thing as failing powers if we look to Mind for our source of supply. The only failure of mind comes from worry and fear—or from disuse.

William James taught that "The more mind does, the more it can do." For its ideas release energy. You can do more and better work than you have ever done. You can know more than you know now. You know from your own experience that under proper mental conditions of joy or enthusiasm you can do three or four times the work without fatigue that you can ordinarily. Tiredness is more boredom than actual physical fatigue. You can work almost indefinitely when the work is a pleasure.

(From *The Secret of the Ages* by Robert Collier, 1926)

ENTHUSIASM IS WEALTH ITSELF

James Allen

Nothing great was ever achieved without enthusiasm.
—RALPH WALDO EMERSON, *CIRCLES*

One of the greatest success methods is to be full of a radiant energy. We are judged every moment by the law of whether we are "the quick or the dead." There are multitudes of dead ones everywhere, and these make the vast army in failure. You may go among the poverty-stricken, the unemployed or the loafing world, and you will find that the quickness of spirit is lacking in them; they are dead to opportunities; dead to enthusiasm; dead to faith; dead in vital understanding and dead to everything that will hold them fast to the great pulsing life current, everywhere waiting their own conscious contact. These failure people are depressed below the level of the universal life—like the Dead Sea or the parched sands of the desert—while within their own being are lying dormant the possibilities of life more abundant and the success that comes from this life.

There are those everywhere who take nothing out of life and who put nothing into it; if it were not that the Heavenly Father feedeth them, they would perish off the earth. There are many people who live in all the beauty of this earth, contacting hourly the wonders of earth, sky, sun, water and verdure, and yet are blind and deaf to all that nature's voice is speaking. "The great wide, beautiful world, with the wonderful waters around it curled, and the wonderful grasses on its breast" are nothing at all to the lives and eyes of the dead ones—they have no value as friends, companions or lovers, for all these associations call for the thrill of the quickening power of sight and sense to make them worthwhile. They have no real value anywhere and are a drag on every situation because they have within them no power of response to any sort of external stimulation. They lack the power to press their own spring of answering enthusiasm and quickness.

Enthusiasm is the dynamics of our personality. Without it, whatever abilities you may possess lie dormant. It is safe to say that all of us have more latent power than we ever learn to use. We may have knowledge, sound judgment and good reasoning facilities, but no one, not even ourselves, will know it until we learn how to put our hearts into thought and action.

POWER, POSSESSIONS AND THE
WHIRLWIND CONSCIOUSNESS

One true eternal success law is enthusiasm. We cannot expect to fan anything into a raging flame of completion unless we do so from the red-hot coals of our own ambition, enthusiasm and aspiration.

Power, possession, attraction, name, fame, honor and success are all the product of a whirlwind consciousness. It is our own life stream that rushes us on past valleys, hills and mountains to deliver our possessions to ourselves, and those who do not generate energy of enthusiasm are at one with the death of their own desires.

It takes a stout heart to always keep enthused in the face of prolonged disappointment and continued opposition, but it must be done if we aim to conquer. There are hours in all business endeavors, in all friendships, all associations, all loves when we must pass along aided alone by our soul's white light and, as Rudyard Kipling said, "When there's nothing in us to hold on to but the power (enthusiasm) which says 'hold on.'" To meet hard places on the path is a part of the great plan, and "We belong to those who go down to the sea in ships and who do business in great waters." And only those who can bid their own lives glow with an enthusiastic radiance will keep light enough to steer past the rocks in the channel.

Not everyone is equally alive in all ways, under all circumstances, and it is as well that we are not or there would no longer be an opportunity to evolve on this planet. It is, however, possible for all of us to have a flaming sword of enthusiasm within us equal to our own development, and no matter how little it may be, it is still there, and like attracts like, for even a grain of mustard seed will move mountains.

USE ENTHUSIASM INSTEAD
OF AN ALARM CLOCK

People who let their enthusiasm awake them in the morning instead of an alarm clock will never fail in business. The managers who let their enthusiasm carry them into an interest in their very lowest employees, to see that labor is comfortable, will never hunt for laborers, nor meet strikes or revolutions. Friends who meet their friends with interest, joy and aliveness will count their friends by the score. And the lovers who give a smile for a smile, truth for truth, heart for a faithful heart will never die alone.

When we study the lives of great men and women, whether they are in the fields of government, business, science or the arts, the one common ingredient all of them possess is enthusiasm about their work and their lives. Enthusiasm enabled Beethoven to compose his great symphonies despite his deafness. Enthusiasm enabled Columbus to persuade Queen Isabella to finance his voyage of discovery and to keep going when it seemed impossible to succeed. Enthusiasm is the secret ingredient of success for the most successful people as well as the generator of happiness in the lives of those who possess it.

With the fire of a great enthusiasm within us we are burning, and we become then a torchbearer and a lamp to the feet of the slumbering multitude. We *are* success then, because we have set the law of our own life and, believing in the law, we come under the protection of the law.

(From *As a Man Thinketh* by James Allen, 1903)

THE MORE SERENITY WE HAVE, THE MORE SUCCESS

James Allen

Remember that there is nothing stable in human affairs; therefore avoid undue elation in prosperity, or undue depression in adversity.

—SOCRATES

Calmness of mind is one of the beautiful jewels of wisdom. It is the result of long and patient effort in self-control. Its presence is an indication of ripened experience, and of a more than ordinary knowledge of the laws and operations of thought.

We become calm in the measure that we understand ourselves as thought-evolved beings, for such knowledge necessitates the understanding of others as the result of thought. As we develop a right understanding, and see more and more clearly the internal relations of things by the action of cause and effect, we cease to fuss and fume and worry and grieve, and remain poised, steadfast, serene.

INFLUENCE AND POWER ARE
BORN IN THE CALM

Calm people, having learned how to govern themselves, know how to adapt themselves to others; and they, in turn, reverence their spiritual strength, and feel that they can learn from them and rely upon them. The more tranquil we become, the greater is our success, our influence and our power for good. Even ordinary merchants will find business prosperity increase as they develop a greater self-control and equanimity, for people will always prefer to deal with people whose demeanor is strongly equable.

Strong, calm people are always loved and revered. They are like a shade-giving tree in a thirsty land, or a sheltering rock in a storm. Who does not love a tranquil heart, a sweet-tempered, balanced life? It does not matter whether it rains or shines, or what changes come to those possessing these blessings, for they are always sweet, serene and calm. That exquisite poise of character, which we call serenity, is the last lesson of culture; it is the flower of life, the fruit of the soul. It is as precious as wisdom. It is more to be desired than gold, more even than fine gold. How insignificant mere money-seeking looks in comparison with a serene life, a life that dwells in the ocean of truth beneath the waves, beyond the reach of tempests in the eternal calm.

How many people do we know who sour their lives, who ruin all that is sweet and beautiful by explosive tempers, who destroy their poise of character and make bad blood? It is a question whether the great majorities of people do not ruin their lives and mar their happiness by lack of self-control. How few people we meet in life who are well balanced, who have that exquisite poise that is characteristic of the finished character!

YOUR CALM, PROSPEROUS THOUGHTS WILL DRIVE YOUR ACTIONS

Yes, humanity surges with uncontrolled passion, is tumultuous with ungoverned grief, is blown about by anxiety and doubt. Only those whose thoughts are controlled and purified make the winds and the storms of the soul obey them.

Tempest-tossed souls, wherever you may be, under whatsoever conditions you may live, know this—in the ocean of life the isles of blessedness are smiling, and the sunny shore of your ideal awaits your coming. This blessedness lies within your own soul. It may be dormant, but you—and only you—can awaken it.

Keep your hand firmly upon the helm of thought. Self-control is strength. Right thought is mastery. Calmness is power. Drive out from your mind evil thoughts, thoughts of illness, thoughts of poverty and thoughts of adversity. Replace them with good thoughts. Think thoughts of achievement. Think thoughts of good deeds. Think thoughts of good health, of prosperity, of happiness. Your thoughts will drive your actions. To paraphrase the words of the Book of Proverbs: "As you think, so shall you be."

(From *As a Man Thinketh* by James Allen, 1903)

THE POWER OF MEDITATION

James Allen

Spiritual meditation is the pathway to Divinity. It is the mystic ladder that reaches from earth to heaven, from error to truth, from pain to peace. Every saint has climbed it; every sinner must sooner or later come to it, and all weary pilgrims who turn their back upon self and the world, and set their faces resolutely toward the Father's Home, must plant their feet upon its golden rounds. Without its aid you cannot grow into the divine state, the divine likeness, the divine peace, and the fadeless glories and nonpolluting joys of truth will remain hidden from you.

Meditation is the intense dwelling, in thought, upon an idea or theme, with the object of thoroughly comprehending it, and whatsoever you constantly meditate upon you will not only come to understand, but will grow more and more into its likeness, for it will become incorporated into your very being, will become, in fact, your very self. If, therefore, you constantly dwell upon that which is selfish and debasing, you will ultimately become selfish and debased; if you ceaselessly think upon that which is pure and unselfish, you will surely become pure and unselfish.

WHAT YOU THINK IS WHERE YOU'RE GOING

Tell me what that is upon which you most frequently and intensely think, that to which, in your silent hours, your soul most naturally turns, and I will tell you to what place of pain or peace you are traveling, and whether you are growing into the likeness of the divine or the bestial.

There is an unavoidable tendency to become literally the embodiment of that quality upon which one most constantly thinks. Let, therefore, the object of your meditation be above and not below, so that every time you revert to it in thought you will be lifted up; let it be pure and unmixed with any selfish element; so shall your heart become purified and drawn nearer to truth, and not defiled and dragged more hopelessly into error.

Meditation, in the spiritual sense in which I am now using it, is the secret of all growth in spiritual life and knowledge. Every prophet, sage and savior became such by the power of meditation. Buddha meditated upon the truth until he could say, "I am the Truth." Jesus brooded upon the Divine imminence until at last he could declare, "I and my Father are One."

PRAYING FOR ONE THING,
THINKING ANOTHER

Meditation centered upon divine realities is the very essence and soul of prayer. It is the silent reaching of the soul toward the Eternal. Mere petitioner prayer without meditation is a body without a soul, and is powerless to lift the mind and heart above sin and affliction. If you are daily praying for wisdom, for peace, for loftier purity and a fuller realization of truth, and that for which you pray is still far from you, it means that you are praying for one thing while living out in thought and act another.

If you will cease from such waywardness, taking your mind off those things you cling to selfishly, which bars you from the possession of the stainless realities for which you pray; if you will no longer ask God to grant you that which you do not deserve, or to bestow upon you that love and compassion which you refuse to bestow upon others, but will commence to think and act in the spirit of truth, you will day by day be growing into those realities, so that ultimately you will become one with them.

If you would secure any worldly advantage, you must be willing to work vigorously for it, and would be foolish indeed to wait with folded hands, expecting it to come to you for the mere asking. Do not then vainly imagine that you can obtain the heavenly possessions without making an effort. Only when you commence to work earnestly in the kingdom of truth will you be allowed to partake of the bread of life, and when you have, by patient and uncomplaining effort, earned the spiritual wages for which you ask, they will not be withheld from you.

NOTHING DREAMY ABOUT MEDITATION

If you really seek truth, and not merely your own gratification; if you love it above all worldly pleasures and gains—more, even, than happiness itself—you will be willing to make the effort necessary for its achievement. If you would be freed from sin and sorrow; if you would taste of that spotless purity for which you sigh and pray; if you would realize wisdom and knowledge, and would enter into the possession of profound and abiding peace, come now and enter the path of meditation, and let the supreme object of your meditation be truth.

At the outset, meditation must be distinguished from idle reverie. There is nothing dreamy and unpractical about it. It is a process of searching and uncompromising thought that allows nothing to remain but the simple and naked truth. Meditating in this way, you will no longer strive to build yourself up in your prejudices, but, forgetting self, you will remember only that you are seeking the truth. And so you will remove, one by one, the errors that you have built around yourself in the past, and will patiently wait for the revelation of truth that will come when your errors have been sufficiently removed.

Select some portion of the day in which to meditate, and keep that period sacred to your purpose. The best time is the very early morning when the spirit of repose is upon everything. All natural conditions will then be in your favor; the passions, after the long bodily fast of the night, will be subdued, the excitements and worries of the previous day will have died away, and the mind, strong and yet restful, will be receptive to spiritual instruction. Indeed, one of the first efforts you will be called upon to make will be to shake off lethargy and indulgence, and if you refuse you will be unable to advance, for the demands of the spirit are imperative.

AN AWAKENED CONSCIOUSNESS,
ALIVE TO POSSIBILITIES

To be spiritually awakened is also to be mentally and physically awakened. The sluggard and the self-indulgent can have no knowledge of truth. If those who are possessed of health and strength waste the calm, precious hours of the silent morning in drowsy indulgence, they are totally unfit to climb the heavenly heights.

Those whose awakening consciousness has become alive to its lofty possibilities, who are beginning to shake off the darkness of ignorance in which the world is enveloped, rise before the stars have ceased their vigil, and, grappling with the darkness within their souls, strive, by holy aspiration, to perceive the light of truth while the unawake world dreams on.

No saint, no holy one, no teacher of truth ever lived who did not rise early in the morning. Jesus habitually rose early, and climbed the solitary mountains to engage in Holy Communion. Buddha always rose an hour before sunrise and engaged in meditation, and all his disciples were enjoined to do the same. "It is well to be up before daybreak, for such habits contribute to health, wealth and wisdom," said Aristotle.

If you have to commence your daily duties at a very early hour, and are thus prevented from giving the early morning to systematic meditation, try to give an hour at night. Should this be denied you, you need not despair, for you may turn your thoughts upward in holy meditation in the intervals of your work, or in those few idle minutes which you now waste in aimlessness. Should your work be of that kind that becomes by practice automatic, you may meditate while engaged upon it. That eminent philosopher Jacob Boehme realized his vast knowledge of divine things while working long hours as a shoemaker. In every life there is time to think, and the busiest, the most laborious is not shut out from aspiration and meditation.

Spiritual meditation and self-discipline are inseparable; you will therefore commence to meditate upon yourself so as to try and understand yourself, for, remember, the great object you will have in view will be the complete removal of all your errors in order that you may realize truth. You will begin to question your motives, thoughts and acts, comparing them with your ideal, and endeavoring to look upon them with a calm and impartial eye.

GAINING MORE AND MORE EQUILIBRIUM

In this manner you will be continually gaining more of that mental and spiritual equilibrium without which men are but helpless straws upon the ocean of life. If you are given to hatred or anger, you will meditate upon gentleness and forgiveness, so as to become actually alive to a sense of your harsh and foolish conduct. You will then begin to dwell in thoughts of love, of gentleness, of abounding forgiveness;

and as you overcome the lower by the higher, there will gradually, silently steal into your heart a knowledge of the divine law of love with an understanding of its bearing upon all the intricacies of life and conduct.

In applying this knowledge to your every thought, word and act, you will grow more and more gentle, more and more loving, more and more divine. And thus with every error, every selfish desire, every human weakness; by the power of meditation is it overcome, and as each sin, each error is thrust out, a fuller and clearer measure of the light of truth illumines the pilgrim soul.

By meditating, you will be ceaselessly fortifying yourself against your only real enemy—your selfish, perishable self—and will be establishing yourself more and more firmly in the divine and imperishable self that is inseparable from truth. The direct outcome of your meditations will be a calm, spiritual strength that will be your stay and resting place in the struggle of life. Great is the overcoming power of holy thought, and the strength and knowledge gained in the hour of silent meditation will enrich the soul with saving remembrance in the hour of strife, of sorrow or of temptation.

As, by the power of meditation, you grow in wisdom, you will relinquish, more and more, your selfish desires, which are fickle, impermanent and productive of sorrow and pain; and will take your stand, with increasing steadfastness and trust, upon unchangeable principles, and will realize heavenly rest.

BECOMING ONE WITH THE ETERNAL

The use of meditation is the acquirement of a knowledge of eternal principles, and the power which results from meditation is the ability to rest upon and trust those principles, and so become one with the Eternal. The end of meditation is, therefore, direct knowledge of truth, God and the realization of divine and profound peace.

Said the divine Gautama, the Buddha, "He who gives himself up to vanity, and does not give himself up to meditation, forgetting the real aim of life and grasping at pleasure, will in time envy him who has exerted himself in meditation." He instructed his disciples in the following "Five Great Meditations":

"The first meditation is the meditation of love, in which you so adjust your heart that you long for the weal and welfare of all beings, including the happiness of your enemies.

"The second meditation is the meditation of pity, in which you think of all beings in distress, vividly representing in your imagination their sorrows and anxieties so as to arouse a deep compassion for them in your soul.

"The third meditation is the meditation of joy, in which you think of the prosperity of others, and rejoice with their rejoicings.

"The fourth meditation is the meditation of impurity, in which you consider the evil consequences of corruption, the effects of sin and diseases. How trivial often the pleasure of the moment, and how fatal its consequences.

"The fifth meditation is the meditation on serenity, in which you rise above love and hate, tyranny and oppression, wealth and want, and regard your own fate with impartial calmness and perfect tranquillity."

By engaging in these meditations, the disciples of the Buddha arrived at knowledge of the truth. But whether you engage in these particular meditations or not matters little so long as your object is truth, so long as you hunger and thirst for that righteousness which is a holy heart and a blameless life. In your meditations, therefore, let your heart grow and expand with ever-broadening love, until, free from all hatred, and passion, and condemnation, it embraces the whole universe with thoughtful tenderness. As the flower opens its petals to receive the morning light, so open your soul more and more to the glorious light of truth. Soar upward upon the wings of aspiration; be fearless, and believe in the loftiest possibilities. Believe that a life of absolute meekness is possible; believe that a life of stainless purity is possible; believe that a life of perfect holiness is possible; believe that the realization of the highest truth is possible. Those who so believe climb rapidly the heavenly hills, while the unbelievers continue to grope darkly and painfully in the fog-bound valleys.

(From *As a Man Thinketh* by James Allen, 1903)

GOING WITHIN: GETTING THE KINKS
OUT OF OUR MINDS AND OUR LIVES

Ralph Waldo Trine

All life is from within out. This is something that cannot be reiterated too often. The springs of life are all from within. This being true, it would be well for us to give more time to the inner life than we are accustomed to give to it, especially in this Western world.

There is nothing that will bring us such abundant returns as to take a little time in the quiet, each day of our lives. We need this to get the kinks out of our minds, and hence out of our lives. We need this to form better the higher ideals of life. We need this in order to see clearly in mind the things upon which we would concentrate and focus our thought-forces.

We need this in order to continually create anew, and to keep our conscious connection with the Infinite. We need this in order that the rush and hurry of our everyday life does not keep us away from the conscious realization of the fact that the spirit of Infinite life and power that is the basis of all—working in and through all, that is the life of all—is the life of our life and the source of our power; and that outside of this we have no life and we have no power.

(From *Character Building Thought Power* by Ralph Waldo Trine, 1900)

THE ESSENTIAL ART OF
RECEIVING RICHES

Ralph Waldo Trine

The method of receiving is not difficult. The principal word to be used is the word "Open."

That means simply to open your mind and heart to the divine inflow, which is waiting only for the opening of the gate so that it may enter. It is no different from opening the gate of the trough that conducts life-giving water from the reservoir above into the field below. The water, by virtue of its very nature, will rush in and irrigate the field, if only the gate has been opened.

In order to open our gate, it is important to realize our Oneness with the Infinite Life and Power that is waiting to supply us with riches. We can do that right now: just realize the intimate relation the Source bears to us and we to It. The open mind and heart is the first thing necessary for an attitude of receiving. The second is an earnest, sincere desire.

OUR GOOD IS THERE IN THE SILENCE

It may be helpful at first to take yourself for a few moments each day into the quiet, into the silence, where you will not be agitated by the disturbances that enter in through the physical senses. There in the quiet, alone with God, put yourself into the receptive attitude. Calmly, quietly and expectantly desire that this realization break in upon and take possession of your soul. As it breaks in upon and takes possession of your soul, it will manifest itself to your mind, and from this you will feel its manifestations in every part of your body.

Then, to the degree that you open yourself to it, you will feel a quiet, peaceful, illuminating power that will harmonize body, soul and mind, and that will then harmonize these with the entire world. You are now on the mountaintop, and the voice of God is speaking to you. Then, as you descend, carry this realization with you. Live in it, waking, working, thinking, walking, sleeping. In this way, although you may not be continually on the mountaintop, you will nevertheless be continually living in the realization of all the beauty, inspiration and power you have felt there.

Moreover, the time will come when in the busy office or on the noisy street you can enter into the silence by simply drawing the mantle of your own thoughts about you and realizing that there and everywhere the Spirit of Infinite Life, Love, Wisdom, Peace, Power and Plenty is guiding, keeping, protecting, leading you. This is the spirit of continual prayer. This is to pray without ceasing. This is to know and to walk with God. This is the new birth, the second, spiritual birth. This is to be swept unto life eternal, whatever one's form of belief or faith may be, for it is life eternal to know God. We will create a new song—"The Beautiful Eternal Now."

This is the realization that you and I can come into this very day, this very hour, this very minute, if we desire and if we will it. And if now we merely set our faces in the right direction, it is then but a matter of time until we come into the full splendor of this complete realization. To set one's face in the direction of the mountain and then simply to journey on, whether rapidly or more slowly, will bring us to it.

But unless we set our face in the right direction and make the start, we will not reach it. It was Goethe who said, "Are you in earnest? Seize this very minute: What you can do, or dream you can, begin it; Boldness has genius, power, and magic in it. Only engage and then the mind grows heated; Begin and then the work will be completed."

(From *In Tune with the Infinite* by Ralph Waldo Trine, 1897)

THE ART OF BEING READY TO RECEIVE

Napoleon Hill

There is a difference between WISHING for a thing and being READY to receive it. **No one is ready for a thing until he believes he can acquire it.** The state of mind must be BELIEF, not mere hope or wish. Open-mindedness is essential for belief. Closed minds do not inspire faith, courage and belief.

Remember, no more effort is required to aim high in life, to demand abundance and prosperity, than is required to accept misery and poverty. A great poet has correctly stated this universal truth through these lines:

> *I bargained with Life for a penny*
> *And Life would pay no more,*
> *However I begged at evening*
> *When I counted my scanty store.*
> *For Life is a just employer,*
> *He gives you what you ask,*
> *But once you have set the wages,*

Why, you must bear the task.
I worked for a menial's hire,
Only to learn, dismayed,
That any wage I had asked of Life,
Life would have willingly paid.

(From *Think and Grow Rich* by Napoleon Hill, 1937)

LET YOUR SOUL EXPAND
INTO PROSPERITY

James Allen

It is granted only to the heart that abounds with integrity, trust, generosity and love to realize true prosperity. The heart that is not possessed of these qualities cannot know prosperity, for prosperity—like happiness—is not an outward possession but an inward realization. Greedy people may become millionaires but they will always be wretched, mean and poor, and will even consider themselves outwardly poor so long as there is another person in the world who is richer than they are. On the other hand, the openhanded and loving will realize a full and rich prosperity, even though their outward possessions may be small.

When we contemplate the fact that the universe is abounding in all good things, material as well as spiritual, and compare it with the blind eagerness to secure a few gold coins or a few acres of dirt, it is then that we realize how dark and ignorant selfishness is. It is then that we know that self-seeking is self-destruction.

Nature gives all, without reservation, and loses nothing; those, grasping all, lose everything. If you would realize true prosperity, do not settle down, as many have done, into the belief that if you do right everything will go wrong. Do not allow the word "competition" to shake your faith in the supremacy of righteousness. I do not care what people may say about the "laws of competition," for I know the unchangeable law, which shall one day put them all to rout, and which puts them to rout even now in the heart and life of the righteous—and knowing this law I can contemplate all dishonesty with undisturbed repose, for I know where certain destruction awaits it.

TRUSTING THE POWER OF THE LAW

Under all circumstances do that which you believe to be right, and trust the law; trust the Divine Power that is imminent in the universe, and it will never desert you, and you will always be protected. By such a trust all your losses will be converted into gains, and all curses that threaten will be transmuted into blessings. Never let go of integrity, generosity and love, for these, coupled with energy, will lift you into the truly prosperous state. Do not believe the world when it tells you that you must always attend to "number one" first, and to others afterward. To do this is not to think of others at all, but only of one's own comforts. To those who practice this the day will come when all will desert them, and when they cry out in their loneliness and anguish there will be no one to hear and help them.

To consider one's self before all others is to cramp, warp and hinder every noble and divine impulse. Let your soul expand, let your heart reach out to others in loving and generous warmth, and great and lasting will be your joy, and all prosperity will come to you.

Those who have wandered from the highway of righteousness guard themselves against competition. Those who always pursue the right do not have to trouble about such defense. This is no empty statement. There are people today who, by the power of integrity and faith, have defied all competition, and who, without swerving in the least from their methods when competed with, have risen steadily into prosperity, while those who tried to undermine them have fallen back defeated.

To possess those inward qualities which constitute goodness is to be armored against all the powers of evil, and to be doubly protected in every time of trial; and to build oneself up in those qualities is to build up a success which cannot be shaken, and to enter into a prosperity which will endure forever.

(From *As a Man Thinketh* by James Allen, 1903)

Part Eight

SOME SIMPLE
PROSPERITY
TECHNIQUES

MENTAL ROADS TO WEALTH

Joseph Murphy

Here is a simple technique you may use to multiply money in your experience. *Use the following statements several times a day:*

I like money. I love it. I use it wisely, constructively and judiciously. Money is constantly circulating in my life. I release it with joy, and it returns to me multiplied in a wonderful way. It is good and very good. Money flows to me in avalanches of abundance. I use it for good only, and I am grateful for my good and for the riches of my mind.

Recognizing the powers of your subconscious mind and the creative power of your thought or mental image is the way to opulence, freedom and constant supply. Accept the abundant life in your own mind. Your mental acceptance and expectancy of wealth has its own mathematics and mechanics of expression. As you enter into the mood of opulence, all things necessary for the abundant life will come to pass.

Let this be your daily affirmation; write it in your heart:

I am one with the infinite riches of my subconscious mind. It is my right to be rich, happy and successful. Money flows to me freely, copiously and endlessly. I am forever conscious of my true worth. I give of my talents freely, and I am wonderfully blessed financially. It is wonderful!

(From *The Power of Your Subconscious Mind* by Joseph Murphy, 1963)

FOURTEEN STEPS TO SUCCESS

Joseph Murphy

1. Be bold enough to claim that it is your right to be rich, and your deeper mind will honor your claim.

2. You don't want just enough to go around. You want all the money you need to do all the things you want to do and when you want to do them. Get acquainted with the riches of your subconscious mind.

3. When money is circulating freely in your life, you are economically healthy. Look at money like the

tide and you will always have plenty of it. The ebb and flow of the tide is constant. When the tide is out, you are absolutely sure that it will return.

4. Knowing the laws of your subconscious mind, you will always be supplied regardless of what form money takes.

5. One reason many people simply make ends meet and never have enough money is that they condemn money. What you condemn takes wings and flies away.

6. Do not make a god of money. It is only a symbol. Remember that the real riches are in your mind. You are here to lead a balanced life—this includes acquiring all the money you need.

7. Don't make money your sole aim. Claim wealth, happiness, peace, true expression and love, and personally radiate love and goodwill to all. Then your subconscious mind will give you compound interest in all these fields of expression.

8. There is no virtue in poverty. It is a disease of the mind, and you should heal yourself of this mental conflict or malady at once.

9. You are not here to live in a hovel, to dress in rags or to go hungry. You are here to lead the life more abundant.

10. Never use the terms "filthy lucre" or "I despise

money." You lose what you criticize. There is nothing good or bad, but thinking of it in either light makes it so.

11. Repeat frequently, "I like money. I use it wisely, constructively and judiciously. I release it with joy, and it returns a thousand fold."

12. Money is not evil any more so than copper, lead, tin or iron which you may find in the ground. All evil is due to ignorance and misuse of the mind's powers.

13. To picture the end result in your mind causes your subconscious to respond and fulfill your mental picture.

14. Stop trying to get something for nothing. There is no such thing as a free lunch. You must give to receive. You must give mental attention to your goals, ideals and enterprises, and your deeper mind will back you up. The key to wealth is application of the laws of the subconscious mind by impregnating it with the idea of wealth.

(From *The Power of Your Subconscious Mind* by Joseph Murphy, 1963)

SIX PROVEN STEPS TO YOUR FORTUNE

Napoleon Hill

The method by which DESIRE for riches can be transmuted into its financial equivalent consists of six definite, practical steps:

First. Fix in your mind the exact amount of money you desire. It is not sufficient merely to say, "I want plenty of money." Be definite as to the amount. (There is a psychological reason for definiteness.)

Second. Determine exactly what you intend to give in return for the money you desire. (There is no such reality as "something for nothing.")

Third. Establish a definite date when you intend to possess the money you desire.

Fourth. Create a definite plan for carrying out your desire, and begin at once—whether you are ready or not—to put this plan into action.

Fifth. Write out a clear, concise statement of the amount of money you intend to acquire; name the time limit for its acquisition; state what you intend to give in return for the money; and describe clearly the plan through which you intend to accumulate it.

Sixth. Read your written statement aloud, twice daily, once just before retiring at night, and once after rising in the morning. AS YOU READ, SEE AND FEEL AND BELIEVE YOURSELF ALREADY IN POSSESSION OF THE MONEY.

It is important that you follow the instructions described in these six steps. It is especially important that you observe and follow the instructions in the sixth paragraph.

You may complain that it is impossible for you to "see yourself in possession of money" before you actually have it. Here is where a BURNING DESIRE will come to your aid. If you truly DESIRE money so keenly that your desire is an obsession, you will have no difficulty in convincing yourself that you will acquire it. The object is to want money, and to become so determined to have it that you CONVINCE yourself you will have it.

Only those who become "money conscious" ever accumulate great riches. "Money consciousness" means that the mind has become so thoroughly saturated with the DESIRE for money that one can see one's self already in possession of it.

To the uninitiated, who has not been schooled in the working principles of the human mind, these instructions may appear impractical. It may be helpful, to all who fail to recognize the soundness of the six steps, to know that the information they convey was received from Andrew Carnegie, who began as an ordinary laborer in the steel mills, but managed, despite his humble beginning, to make these principles yield him a fortune of considerably more than one hundred million dollars.

It may be of further help to know that the six steps here recommended were carefully scrutinized by Thomas A. Edison, who placed his stamp of approval upon them as being not only the steps essential for the accumulation of money, but necessary for the attainment of any definite goal.

The steps call for no "hard labor." They call for no sacrifice. They do not require one to become ridiculous or credulous. To apply them does not require a great amount of education. But the successful application of these six steps does call for sufficient imagination to enable one to see, and to understand, that accumulation of money cannot be left to chance, good fortune and luck. One must realize that all who have accumulated great fortunes first did a certain amount of dreaming, hoping, wishing, DESIRING and PLANNING before they acquired money.

You may as well know, right here, that you can never have riches in great quantities UNLESS you can work yourself into a white heat of DESIRE for money, and actually BELIEVE you will possess it.

(From *Think and Grow Rich* by Napoleon Hill, 1937)

THE CREATIVE POWER OF OPTIMISM

Gregg Easterbrook of the Brookings Institute has reported the results of studies proving that optimistic people, even though they're aware that the world is full of problems, live longer and have higher incomes and longer marriages. They also suffer fewer strokes and less depression.

More than a hundred years before this report was issued, Ralph Waldo Trine (*In Tune with the Infinite*) was writing that "The Optimist has the power of seeing things in their entirety and in their right relations." He said this sight is aided by the optimist's understanding, illuminated by wisdom, whereas the pessimist is illuminated by ignorance. "The optimists are making their own heaven," he said, "and to the degree that they make their own heaven are they helping to make one for all the world, beside." Christian D. Larson agreed.

THE OPTIMIST CREED

Christian D. Larson

To be so strong that nothing can disturb your peace
of mind.

To talk health, happiness and prosperity to every person
you meet.

To make all your friends feel that there is something
worthwhile in them.

To look on the sunny side of everything and make your
optimism come true.

To think only of the best, to work only for the best, and
to expect only the best.

To be just as enthusiastic about the success of others as
you are about your own.

To forget the mistakes of the past and press on to the
greater achievements of the future.

To wear a cheerful expression at all times and give a smile
to every living creature you meet.

To give so much time to improving yourself that you have
no time to criticize others.

To be too large for worry, too noble for anger, too strong for
   fear, and too happy to permit the presence of trouble.
To think well of yourself and to proclaim this fact to the
   world, not in loud words but in great deeds.
To live in the faith that the whole world is on your side,
   so long as you are true to the best that is in you.

(From *Your Forces and How to Use Them* by Christian D. Larson, 1912)

APPENDIX

Napoleon Hill (1883–1970)

Think and Grow Rich is not only Napoleon Hill's most famous book but it's also the bestselling success book of all time. More than 45 million copies of Napoleon Hill's books have been sold worldwide. They are all practical, easy to read and universally recognized as the foundation for all contemporary motivational thinking. After all, Hill motivated the entire Western world with the speechwriting he did for FDR, including the line "We have nothing to fear but fear itself."

The luster of the name Napoleon Hill has never dimmed. Insert that name into an Amazon book search today and nearly 18,000 references come up. Why? Because the motivational guru never fails to be quoted in books whose subjects are as wide-ranging as diet, the pentathlon, communication, simple abundance, JFK, teens, online trading, feng shui, leadership, taking a band on the road, Zen and countless more. *Think and Grow Rich* has been called "the granddaddy of all motivational literature." It was the first book to boldly ask, "What makes a winner?" The man who asked and listened for the answer, Napoleon Hill, is now counted in the top ranks of the world's winners himself. In the original *Think and Grow Rich*, Hill tells the stories of Andrew Carnegie, Thomas Edison, Henry Ford and other millionaires of his generation to illustrate his principles.

Dr. Joseph Murphy (1898–1981)

Joseph Murphy wrote, taught, counseled and lectured to thousands all over the world for nearly 50 years. He wrote more than 30 books, including *The Amazing Laws of Cosmic Mind*, *Secrets of the I-Ching*, *The Miracle of Mind Dynamics*, *Your Infinite Power to Be Rich* and *The Cosmic Power Within You*. His most noted work, *The Power of Your Subconscious Mind*, has sold millions of copies and continues to sell all over the world.

Dr. Murphy teaches the simple, scientifically proven techniques and the astonishing facts about how your subconscious powers can perform miracles of healing. How lung cancer has been cured and optic nerves made whole again. How you can use the newly discovered Law of Attraction to increase your money-getting powers. How your subconscious mind can win you friends, peace of mind, and even help you to attract the ideal mate. How your dreams can help you solve problems and make difficult decisions—or warn you of potential disaster. Prosperity, happiness and perfect health are yours when you use *The Power of Your Subconscious Mind*.

Murphy saw the subconscious mind as a darkroom within which we develop the images that are to be lived out in real life. While the conscious mind sees an event, takes a picture of it and remembers it, the subconscious mind works backward, "seeing" something before it happens (why intuition is infallible). "The law of your mind is the law of belief itself," Murphy said. "What we believe makes us who we are."

Orison S. Marden (1850–1924)

"We lift ourselves by our thought. We climb upon our vision of ourselves."

More than 3 million books by the legendary O. S. Marden, the founder of today's popular *Success Magazine*, have been sold to date. Dr. Marden is widely considered to be the forerunner of such writers and thinkers as Napoleon Hill, Earl Nightingale, Og Mandino, Norman Vincent Peale and Tony Robbins. "I would list him among such great writers as Thoreau, Emerson, Dale Carnegie and Horatio Alger—all positive thinkers," wrote Reverend Peale to Marden's widow.

Reverend Robert Schuller called Dr. Marden's writings "inspired and specific."

Considered to be the founder of the modern success movement in America, Marden successfully bridged the gap between the old, narrow notions of success and the new, more comprehensive models made popular by the best-selling authors who came later and are still writing.

Ezra Taft Benson, thirteenth president of the Mormon Church, wrote that he started on the road to greatness when his grandparents gave him Orison S. Marden's two-volume set of writings, which he "devoured." Marden's reputation remained undiminished through the years, his influence threaded throughout American thoughts and writings. Today, for instance, the Internet's Direct Selling Masterclass draws participants with Marden's words, along with the words of Churchill, Roosevelt, Malcolm Forbes and Zig Ziglar.

Marden was famous for good reason. His beliefs spur us on; his clear convictions make it impossible for the human mind and heart not to respond: "Our destiny changes with our thought. We shall become what we wish to become, do what we wish to do, when our habitual thought corresponds with our desire."

Theron Q. Dumont (1862–c. 1932)

It is widely assumed that William Walker Atkinson is another name used by Theron Q. Dumont. William Walker

Atkinson, in all his incarnations, was a star player in the early days of the New Thought movement. A lawyer turned metaphysician, he lived in Chicago around the turn of the century, writing many books, both under his own name and, when the subject was yoga, under the name Swami Ramacharaka, another pen name. Atkinson was so practiced in yoga that his books were warmly received in India.

One of Atkinson's subjects was "mental science," as it was then known. In 1889 an article by him titled "A Mental Science Catechism" appeared in a new periodical, *Modern Thought*. He later assumed editorship of *New Thought*. During these years he built for himself an enduring place in the hearts of its readers, as article after article of strength and vital force flowed from his pen.

Atkinson wrote a great many books on New Thought, all of which became very popular and influential among New Thought devotees and practitioners and achieved wide circulation. From 1916 to 1919 he edited the journal *Advanced Thought*, and was for a time honorary president of the International New Thought Alliance. William Walker Atkinson is best known for clarifying the most perplexing scientific and metaphysical teachings, and for his effective comparisons of different schools of logic, ethics and religion.

Christian D. Larson (1874–c. 1932)

Christian D. Larson was famous for his encouraging concept of "the ideal made real." Larson was an outstanding New

Thought leader and teacher. A prolific writer of New Thought books, Larson believed that people have tremendous latent powers that, with the proper attitude, could all be harnessed for success.

The New Thought movement in Cincinnati, Ohio, owes its origin to Larson, who organized the New Thought Temple there in January 1910. In September of that year Mr. Larson began to publish *Eternal Progress*, for several years one of the leading New Thought periodicals.

Larson strode into the spotlight in 1912, when he wrote "The Optimist Creed" that appeared in his book *Your Forces and How to Use Them*. It was adapted as the Optimist International's Creed in 1922. Many have found inspiration in The Creed, which has been used in hospitals to speed patients' recovery, and in locker rooms, where coaches have used it to motivate their players. One of Christian D. Larson's main claims to fame lies in the influence he had on Ernest Holmes, founder of one of the major worldwide branches of New Thought, Religious Science, also known as Science of Mind.

Arnold Bennett (1867–1931)

Arnold Bennett "was indubitably great," wrote Rebecca West. Somerset Maugham agreed and explained why: "All his books bear proof of an extremely penetrating vision regarding his fellow creatures." Bennett's *Old Wife's Tale* is on every short list of the Western world's greatest novels, but what many of today's readers don't know is that Bennett was also enormously successful with his Philosophy for Living series—what he called his "Pocket Philosophies"—where he employed that penetrating vision every bit as well as he did in his fiction. Margaret Drabble, one of Bennett's biographers, wrote about "the role Bennett was to play in educating the taste of the English public, in castigating it, in the most amiable and persuasive fashion, for its philistinism." One of the ways he did that was with these enormously popular little books, seven in all, that expanded his reputation far beyond readers of fiction.

These volumes comprise what many consider to be the first series of self-help books ever published. In them Bennett gave thoughtful, direct, clearly written advice about living—advice that is as relevant today as ever. *How to Live on 24 Hours a Day* was a major bestseller for Bennett in England and the United States. He reported that the book "brought me more letters of appreciation than all of my other books put together." During a tour of the United States in 1911, he met admiring readers of this first time-management book wherever he went, and was even told that medical doctors were prescribing the book for their patients.

American business leaders were especially taken with the Philosophy for Living series. Henry Ford told Bennett in 1930 that he had once bought 500 copies of *How to Live on 24 Hours a Day* to give to his employees, and Ralston Purina founder William Danforth enthusiastically recommends the book in his inspirational classic, *I Dare You!*

James Allen (1864–1912)

"As you may have previously woven in ignorance and pain, may you now weave in enlightenment and happiness."

There has to be a certain truth and magic in a book that has remained in print, selling steadily, for more than a hundred years. James Allen's *As a Man Thinketh* is one of those rare works. This is an inspired outpouring of indisputable truth and self-empowerment. The reasons it endures are obvious.

In the words of one of today's Amazon.com online reader/reviewers: "As these simple yet brilliantly shining words of James Allen have seeped slowly into my subconscious, my life has slowly and steadily changed for the better. I have ceased doing the things I don't want to do in life; I spend my time doing what I love. I have written successful books and recorded albums of my music. I have created a successful business. I have discovered my purpose in life."

This crucial inspirational book has influenced millions. James Allen starts us thinking—even when we would rather be doing something else: "Cherish your visions; cherish your ideas; cherish the music that stirs in your heart, the beauty that forms in your mind, the loveliness that drapes your purest thoughts, for out of them will grow delightful conditions and a heavenly environment."

Julia Seton, M.D. (1862–1950)

Dr. Julia Seton was one of the most outstanding women of the late nineteenth and early twentieth centuries, one of the very few women physicians of her time and a revered member of the original New Thought Alliance. One of the first women to be accepted into the American Medical Association, she wrote many articles for the *Journal of the AMA*, and devoted her life to helping people cope not only with their health problems, but also with the way they lived their lives. Early in her career Dr. Seton recognized the close relationship between one's physical well-being and one's attitude toward life, becoming a pioneer in what today is called the holistic approach to healthy living.

Dr. Seton was a dynamic speaker at the San Francisco World Fair, and set up what she called New Civilization Centers all over the world, working tirelessly to bring New Thought abroad. She was a prolific writer whose essays, articles and poems were widely published. *Concentration* was published first in 1909 and reissued in 1912. Julia Seton's books were precursors of such self-help books as those written by Dale Carnegie, Norman Vincent Peale and Napoleon Hill in the decades that followed.

Robert Collier (1885–1950)

Robert Collier's inspirational books have changed the lives of thousands. He was a prolific New Thought writer who strongly believed that happiness and abundance were within easy reach for everyone. For a long time he had the idea for a set of books on practical psychology. He put this idea into action, working night and day writing the series of seven books. Within six months of the books being published, he received more than 1 million dollars' worth of orders for them. The books were entitled *The Secret of the Ages*. He sold more than 300,000 sets of the books and received thousands of letters telling of positive results obtained from reading his series.

Robert Collier wrote four more books, which he sold separately as *The God in You*, *The Secret Power*, *The Magic Word* and *The Law of the Higher Potential*. He later combined this excellent material into one book and named it *The Law of the Higher Potential*. It has since been renamed *Riches Within Your Reach*.

Ralph Waldo Trine (1866–1958)

"Within yourself lies the cause of whatever enters into your life. The full realization of your own awakened interior powers is to be able to condition your life in exact accord with what you would have."

Henry Ford made no bones about it. He would give credit to the one book that inspired his phenomenal success: *In Tune with the Infinite*. But Ford was not the only one inspired by this small but mighty work. This classic book inspired a generation, selling more than 2 million copies. It is thought to be the original work of inspirational writing that led to such bestsellers as *Think and Grow Rich* and *The Power of Positive Thinking*.

Ralph Waldo Trine was a tremendously popular pioneer when it came to writing about the power of human thought to transform our lives. No other author writing on the subject sold more books and was more successful in extending the reach of the New Thought message to the general public. His remarkable, seminal book, *In Tune with the Infinite* has stood the test of time for well over a century. The message of this book is dynamically simple: the central fact of human life is its connection with the infinite power beyond the universe, and making solid that connection means a free flow of abundance, personal blessings, intuitive knowledge and a strong sense of well-being.

Wallace D. Wattles (1860–1911)

There are few facts known about Wallace Delois Wattles's life, but what is known is inspirational and impressive. Some say he was born during the Civil War, some say just after, but we know he was born an American in 1860. During his relatively brief life of faith and struggle, he experienced a great deal of what most of us would call "failure." Now, in hindsight, it is clear that in order to teach us how to climb out of lesser circumstances, he chose to undergo that trial himself. That he did, mastering his thought and his practice of visualization to such an extent that he died well-off, able to provide for his family in the manner that became his ideal and his image. His inspirations ranged from Descartes and Spinoza to Swedenborg and Emerson, whose ideas he worked with as a foundation for his own solid, practical New Thought principles.

Wattles's books included *Health Through New Thought and Fasting*, *The Science of Being Great*, *The Science of Being Well*, and a novel, *Hellfire Harrison*. He is best known for his prosperity classic, *The Science of Getting Rich*.

ACKNOWLEDGMENTS

JMW Group wishes to acknowledge, with deepest gratitude, the eleven great leaders in success whose experience and wisdom have provided the material for this book. Discovering—and proving—the certain way to wealth, they taught their secrets and strategies to others through the inspired writings that are excerpted here. These eleven founding geniuses of the self-help movement are James Allen, Arnold Bennett, Robert Collier, Theron Q. Dumont, Napoleon Hill, Christian D. Larson, Orison S. Marden, Dr. Joseph Murphy, Julia Seton, Ralph Waldo Trine and Wallace D. Wattles. Brief biographies of these great leaders in success are included in the appendix.

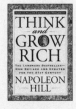

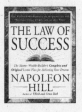

The Master-Key to Riches by Napoleon Hill
The actual handbook that Napoleon Hill gave to teachers of his ideas—a master class from the greatest motivational writer of all time. Revised and updated.   ISBN 978-1-58542-709-3

The Magic Ladder to Success by Napoleon Hill
Napoleon Hill's distillation of a lifetime of ideas in a compact, powerful primer. Revised and updated.   ISBN 978-1-58542-710-9

Your Magic Power to Be Rich! by Napoleon Hill
A three-in-one resource, featuring revised and updated editions of the classics *Think and Grow Rich; The Master-Key to Riches;* and *The Magic Ladder to Success.*   ISBN 978-1-58542-555-6

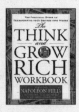
The Think and Grow Rich Workbook
The do-it-yourself workbook for activating Napoleon Hill's winning principles in your life.
ISBN 978-1-58542-711-6

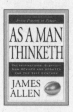

As a Man Thinketh by James Allen
Revised and updated for the twenty-first century,
this is one of the world's most widely loved
inspirational works—as a special bonus it includes
an updated edition of the author's first book, *From
Poverty to Power.*   ISBN 978-1-58542-638-6

The Secret of the Ages by Robert Collier
The classic on how to attain the life you want—
through the incredible visualizing faculties of
your mind.   ISBN 978-1-58542-629-4

The Master Key System by Charles F. Haanel
The legendary guide on how to enact the
"Law of Attraction" in your life.
ISBN 978-1-58542-627-0

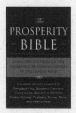

The Prosperity Bible
This beautiful boxed volume features complete
classics by Napoleon Hill, Benjamin Franklin,
James Allen, Florence Scovel Shinn, Ernest
Holmes, and many others.   ISBN 978-1-58542-614-0

A Message to Garcia by Elbert Hubbard
History's greatest motivational lesson, now collected with Elbert Hubbard's most treasured inspirational writings in a signature volume.
ISBN 978-1-58542-691-1

The Science of Getting Rich by Wallace D. Wattles
The time-tested program for a life of prosperity—features the rare bonus work "How to Get What You Want."   ISBN 978-1-58542-601-0

Public Speaking for Success by Dale Carnegie
The definitive, complete edition of Dale Carnegie's public-speaking bible—now revised and updated.   ISBN 978-1-58542-492-4

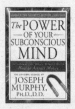

The Power of Your Subconscious Mind by Joseph Murphy, Ph.D., D.D.
The complete, original edition of the million-selling self-help guide that reveals your invisible power to attain any goal.   ISBN 978-1-58542-768-0